the Smoke Shop®

BACKYARD

BBQ

ANDY HUSBANDS

AND

WILL SALAZAR

© 2020 Quarto Publishing Group USA Inc.
Text © 2020 Andy Husbands
Photography © 2020 Ken Goodman

First Published in 2020 by Fair Winds Press, an imprint of The Quarto Group,
100 Cummings Center, Suite 265-D, Beverly, MA 01915, USA.
T (978) 282-9590 F (978) 283-2742 QuartoKnows.com

Fair Winds Press titles are also available at discount for retail, wholesale, promotional, and bulk purchase. For details, contact the Special Sales Manager by email at specialsales@quarto.com or by mail at The Quarto Group, Attn: Special Sales Manager, 100 Cummings Center, Suite 265-D, Beverly, MA 01915, USA.

24 23 22 21 20   1 2 3 4 5
ISBN: 978-1-59233-902-0

Digital edition published in 2020

eISBN: 978-1-63159-762-6
Library of Congress Cataloging-in-Publication Data

Names: Husbands, Andy, author. | Salazar, Will, author.

Title: The smoke shop cookbook : eat, drink, and party like a pit master / Andy Husbands, Will Salazar.

Description: Beverly : Fair Winds Press, 2020.

Identifiers: LCCN 2019033092 (print) | LCCN 2019033093 (ebook) | ISBN 9781592339020 (hardcover) | ISBN 9781631597626 (ebook)

Subjects: LCSH: Barbecuing. | LCGFT: Cookbooks.

Classification: LCC TX840.B3 H8658 2020 (print) | LCC TX840.B3 (ebook) | DDC 641.7/6--dc23

LC record available at https://lccn.loc.gov/2019033092

LC ebook record available at https://lccn.loc.gov/2019033093

Design & Layout: Tanya Jacobson, jcbsn.co

Cover Image: Ken Goodman

Photography: Ken Goodman, page 214 Shutterstock

Food Stylist: Catrine Kelty

Printed in China

DEDICATION

FOR OUR DAUGHTERS
MILLICENT, ESTER, AND AMELIA

BACKYARD BBQ

EAT, DRINK, AND PARTY LIKE A PITMASTER

ANDY HUSBANDS — AND — **WILL SALAZAR**

FAIR WINDS

CONTENTS

A TOAST
FROM ————————————
MICHAEL SYMON

I'VE ALWAYS LOVED ANDY AND WILL'S APPROACH TO FOOD.

They both take everything that they've learned as classically trained chefs and put it together with their passion for all things barbecue. Then they add their own personal food memories—Andy's from growing up in Washington State and summering in New England and Will's from his childhood in Florida.

That combination is what makes The Smoke Shop a truly magical experience. Andy and Will know that barbecue is never just about the food. Great barbecue is about food and fun and family.

I'm reminded of that every time I'm lucky enough to get to The Smoke Shop. There's an energy and happiness in the dining room and in the kitchen. Every bite of barbecue makes you more excited about the next bite and the conversations that will follow it.

You'll feel that same energy—it's love, really—as you try the amazing recipes in this cookbook. So, fire up your pit, make yourself one of these fabulous cocktails, and get in your most comfortable chair to tell and listen to your favorite stories. It's time to party like a pit master!

———

MICHAEL SYMON
JAMES BEARD AWARD–WINNING CHEF

MEET ANDY
AND WILL

////////////////////////

"BARBECUE IS THE FRIENDLIEST FOOD."

—WORLD CHAMPION PIT MASTER
TUFFY STONE

SAY THE WORD "BARBECUE" AND SOME PEOPLE WILL THINK "SMOKED MEAT" AND OTHERS WILL THINK "PARTY!" WE THINK THAT EVERYBODY IS RIGHT—AND THAT'S WHAT THIS BOOK IS ABOUT: GREAT FOOD AND GOOD TIMES. WE TAKE BARBECUE (THE SMOKED MEAT) PRETTY SERIOUSLY, BUT WE THINK BARBECUE (THE PARTY) SHOULD BE NOTHING BUT A CELEBRATION, FOR BOTH THE PIT MASTER AND THE GUESTS.

"We" are Andy Husbands and Will Salazar, the founder and the culinary director of The Smoke Shop restaurant, where we turn out over half a million pounds of smoked meat and throw a party 363 days a year. We're a little reluctant to do the math, but between us, we've been throwing parties almost every day for fifty years—in restaurants and, on our precious days off, at our own homes.

Tuffy, who we quoted right up there, is a friend, and, yes, Andy got to know him over barbecue. They competed in some of the country's fiercest BBQ competitions. But Tuffy knows what he's talking about there: Even when bragging rights are at stake, barbecue is the friendliest food. It's not that pit masters are inherently nicer people—there's definitely a lot of ego involved when it comes to being

the best—but the process of smoking a perfect brisket, well, it takes time, and it's better to pass that time with a good talker, preferably one who's got a cooler of beers or fine whiskey. That sense of community is what hooked Andy on barbecue at his first-ever competition. It was pouring rain, cold, and muddy, and the team didn't even have the right equipment, but a pit master named Uncle Jed invited them in for a bourbon and to warm up by the smoker. Generosity is the soul of barbecue—and that's why you'll see other pit masters, chefs, bartenders, and butchers throughout this book sharing their barbecue party knowledge.

It's that feeling of food and friends and family Andy remembers from grilling country-style ribs with his father in their backyard in Washington State as a kid.

They'd cook them over cheap charcoal briquettes doused in a ton of lighter fluid and drench them in KC Masterpiece. It's still a flavor—and a fond memory—Andy craves. (His ode to the supermarket favorite BBQ sauce is on page 33.)

Then, of course, there's the amount of meat involved in barbecue. Cows and pigs—they are big animals and the classic barbecue cuts aren't sized for one or two people. You throw on a couple of racks of ribs—and if you are standing by a smoker for hours, why wouldn't you smoke as many racks as you can fit—or a Boston butt for pulled pork and suddenly you have food for a dozen or more. Simply put, you need friends for barbecue, not because the cooking itself requires an extra pair of hands, but because the eating does. Barbecue is for sharing.

That's always been Will's experience. For him, barbecue is a warm hug from his grandmother. When he was a kid, the family would gather at Granny's house in Jacksonville, Florida, everyone hanging around the smoker, talking, or picking zucchini and tomatoes and green beans in the garden, talking. There was always a feast: macaroni and cheese, squash casserole, tomato pie, and, of course, his grandfather's chicken. If Grandpa was making chicken, everyone was sure to be there. (Will's tribute to his grandpa's recipe is on page 21. And of course, we've got sides, too.)

It's all a little different in a restaurant, of course, but the basics don't change. We've got a rule at The Smoke Shop: "Treat everyone like Grandma." Actually, Andy used say, "Treat everyone like your mother-in-law." He really likes his mother-in-law, so he was shocked to discover that not everyone can say the same thing. But Grandma? Everyone understands that Granny deserves respect and love. That's how we think about our service and about our food—and about this cookbook.

Barbecue is smoked meat *and* it's a party. It's a cooking technique *and* a way of looking at the world. In this book, we want to give you the recipe for all of that. A way to capture all the best of the barbecue in a big country backyard or on a small city balcony, whether you are serving up a classic BBQ buffet, a casual Taco Tuesday spread, or an extravagant holiday gathering. Any gathering can be a barbecue with respect and love and a little smoke.

OUR PARTY GUESTS

This might be unexpected, from two chefs, but we believe the most important part of a party isn't the food. It's the people you share it with. Here are some of the other people you'll meet in the pages of this cookbook.

JEREMY SEWALL

You might not expect a caviar expert at a barbecue, but Jeremy Sewall has the soul of a pitmaster: he knows everything there is to know about fish eggs, but he isn't fussy. The chef, restaurant owner, and cookbook author just wants to share his knowledge and—lucky for us—his favorite caviar choices (page 206) with everyone at the party. No mother-of-pearl spoon required—but we do recommend some BBQ chips (page 178).

MICHAEL BOUGHTON

Michael will be the one at the party with a negroni in hand. It's his go-to for a gathering: just a few ingredients (equal parts gin, sweet vermouth, and Campari) that add up to a memorable cocktail. He's the beverage director at The Smoke Shop, so he certainly knows his way around a bar, but for a party, he always keeps things simple. "The cocktail should be fun," he says. The recipes he created for this book embrace that cook-friendly approach.

GARRETT HARKER

We always expect Garrett to bring the wine and the oysters to the party. He owns several seafood restaurants in New England and is a pro at shucking fresh bivalves. Wine is a passion for him, but he doesn't take grapes too seriously. His advice on choosing a bottle of wine: "Choose something personal." Maybe a wine from a region you've traveled to. Garrett's not one to drone on about wine, but we love to hear stories from his trips. (Get more wine tips from Garrett on page 181.)

SARAH MCKNIGHT

For years, our most-sought-after invite was Sarah McKnight's annual dessert party. Sarah's an expert baker, and in the depths of winter, she'd celebrate sugar with a dozen different cakes and pastries, plus cookies, because, as she says, "cookies don't count." The dessert buffet went by the wayside when Sarah became a mom, but she shared some of her favorite recipe for our parties, including her most-requested Derby Slab Bars (page 182).

TANIYA NAYAK

Taniya can turn any meal into a party with a well-placed centerpiece or her current favorite flourish, a fancy old silver serving tray she coated with chalkboard paint to serve as the evening's menu board. For a big party, the HGTV and Food Network star will encourage her guests to get into the mood by dressing to the theme. (Taniya has more ideas on page 152.) We think the Macon Mule she requested for a Derby party (page 152) is more than enough reason to dress in seersucker and oversize hats.

RONNIE SAVENOR

Any question we ever have about meat, we turn to Ronnie—and you'll see his answers throughout this book. His family has run Savenor's Market, the premier butcher shop in the Boston area, for eighty years. Want proof that it's the best? This is where Julia Child shopped. On your behalf, we asked Ronnie the most important question of all: How can everyone find a butcher as good as he is? "Look for someone you trust," he says. "And a butcher shop that doesn't smell like anything at all."

THE BACKYARD
BBQ

THE BACKYARD BARBECUE MIGHT JUST BE THE PERFECT PARTY. WE THINK OF IT AS CLASSIC ROCK—EVERYBODY KNOWS IT, EVERYBODY LIKES IT, AND THEY'LL PROBABLY SING ALONG. (ESPECIALLY AFTER SOME CHARRED CAYENNE LEMONADE WITH A KICK, PAGE 44.) FOR THE GUESTS, A BACKYARD BARBECUE IS EASY, COMFORTABLE, AND FAMILIAR. AND FOR THE COOKS, IT'S NICE TO KNOW THAT IF YOUR NEIGHBOR SHOWS UP UNANNOUNCED, THERE'S ALWAYS PLENTY OF FOOD TO GO AROUND.

Think of the food as the foundation for this party, not the focus. It's the excuse to bring people together. Barbecue classics like pulled chicken and pit beans are great for the buffet table because they are good right off the smoker and just as good an hour later when that fierce game of cornhole or horseshoes is over.

Slow-cooked ribs—like the New Memphis Ribs in this chapter (page 28)—are a must for a warm, sunny day in the backyard, says Andy. It's a dish you don't get all the time, a reminder that this moment is something special. And there's no better compliment to the cook than a smile covered in barbecue sauce. For Will, it's all about the sides. Growing up in the South, every party seemed to be a potluck.

He's not sure he's ever been to a barbecue that didn't have mac and cheese and coleslaw on offer. You should invite him over to your next bash. He just might bring Baked Macaroni & Cheese with Bacon and Asparagus (page 38).

One tip from a couple of guys who have catered countless backyard barbecue: The meat is always better when it has time to relax after it comes off the smoker. And the cooks are always better when they have time to relax, too. Give yourself a few minutes before everyone shows up to sit down at the picnic table and open a beer. It doesn't get much better than this.

CLASSIC PULLED PORK

ACTIVE TIME: 30 MINUTES

TOTAL TIME: 12 TO 14 HOURS

SERVES: 12 TO 14

INGREDIENTS

- 10- to 12-pound (4.6 to 5.5 kg) bone-in pork butt (Boston butt)
- ½ cup (75 g) plus 2 tablespoons (18 g) Basic Pork BBQ Rub, divided (page 32)
- 1¼ cups (295 ml) white grape juice
- 2 tablespoons (28 ml) apple cider vinegar
- 1 cup (235 ml) North Carolina Vinegar Sauce (page 20) or ½ cup (120 ml) Bare-Bones BBQ Sauce (page 35) mixed with ½ cup (120 ml) apple cider vinegar

SPECIAL EQUIPMENT

- Smoker and accessories (see page 212)
- Post oak or your favorite hardwood
- Probe thermometer
- Spray bottle
- Neoprene gloves
- Nitrate gloves
- Cooler, for holding meat

YOU CAN'T MAKE PULLED PORK IN A SLOW COOKER. YOU JUST CAN'T. REAL BARBECUED PULLED PORK HAS AN INTENSELY CARAMELIZED EXTERIOR—WHAT PIT MASTERS CALL BARK—AND JUICY CHUNKS OF MEAT. THE KEY TO THAT JUICINESS IS COOKING THE MEAT BONE-IN AND PULLING THE MEAT NO MORE THAN 15 MINUTES BEFORE YOU PLAN TO SERVE IT. OTHERWISE, THE MEAT WILL BECOME DRY AND STRINGY. THE PERFECT BITE MIXES PORK, MEAT JUICES, VINEGARY SAUCE, AND SOME OF THAT SWEET, SAVORY, AND SALTY BARK.

METHOD

Remove the Boston butt from the refrigerator about 1 hour before smoking. Lightly and evenly coat the meat with ½ cup (75 g) of the rub.

Preheat your smoker to 250°F (121°C). About 30 minutes before you are ready to cook, stoke the fire with hardwood; we prefer post oak. (See page 212 for additional information on preparing a smoker.)

Insert the thermometer probe into the center of the Boston butt. Place the meat in your smoker.

Keep your smoker at a constant 250°F (121°C) for the duration of your cook, regularly adding wood or coals. Smoke for 3 hours.

Meanwhile, in a spray bottle, combine the grape juice and vinegar. After 3 hours, evenly spray all sides of the meat once each hour.

After 12 to 14 hours, when the pork butt has reached an internal temperature of 202°F (94°C), remove it from the smoker using neoprene gloves. To serve immediately, rest the meat on a wire rack for 15 minutes. Using neoprene gloves, remove the bone (it should slide out easily). Using nitrate gloves, shred the meat with your hands, mixing in the juice of the meat. If you are waiting to serve the meat, prepare a tempered cooler by filling the cooler with warm water. Close the lid and wait 10 minutes. Remove the water, place the meat in the warm cooler, and close the lid. You can store the meat for up to 2 hours before removing the bone and shredding.

When you are ready to serve, lightly dress the shredded pork with the North Carolina Vinegar Sauce and dust with the remaining 2 tablespoons (18 g) of rub.

STORAGE

Wrap tightly in plastic wrap and refrigerate for up to 4 days or freeze for up to 1 month.

NORTH CAROLINA VINEGAR SAUCE

ACTIVE TIME: 15 MINUTES
TOTAL TIME: 15 MINUTES
YIELD: 2 CUPS (475 ML)

ANDY HAS TRAVELED ALL OVER THE CAROLINAS EATING BARBECUE. ALONG THE WAY, HE'S TASTED SOME AMAZING CLASSIC NORTH CAROLINA VINEGAR SAUCES—BUT THIS ISN'T ONE OF THEM. THIS RECIPE BUILDS ON THAT TRADITION WITH A KICK OF SOUTHEAST ASIAN HOT SAUCE. USE IT TO ACCENTUATE THE FLAVOR OF ALMOST ANYTHING—PULLED PORK, GRILLED STEAK, EVEN FISH AND CHIPS. THE SAUCE IS BEST MADE A FEW DAYS AHEAD OF TIME.

INGREDIENTS

- 1 cup (235 ml) apple cider vinegar
- 1 cup (235 ml) white vinegar
- 2 tablespoons (30 g) light brown sugar
- 1 tablespoon (15 g) ketchup
- 1 tablespoon (15 ml) Frank's RedHot, Louisiana Hot Sauce, or Texas Pete Original Hot Sauce
- 1½ teaspoons kosher salt
- 1 teaspoon blackstrap molasses
- 1 tablespoon (15 ml) sriracha or (15 g) sambal olek
- 1 teaspoon coarsely ground black pepper
- 1 teaspoon red pepper flakes

METHOD

Combine all the ingredients in a small saucepan over medium-high heat. Bring to a simmer, stirring occasionally until everything is melted and incorporated, about 5 minutes. Remove from the heat and cool to room temperature. Transfer the sauce to a container with a tight-fitting lid and shake well before using.

STORAGE

Refrigerate in an airtight container indefinitely.

WHAT THE BUTCHER KNOWS:

PORK BUTT

WHAT IT IS: Also known as Boston butt, this is not the pig's behind, but the thickest part of the animal's shoulder, with the bone in. ("Butt" can mean the thicker end of something, as in the butt of a gun.)

WHAT TO ASK FOR: You want a well-marbled, bone-in pork butt or Boston butt, known among butchers as NAMP #406. For the best marbling, you'll want a heritage breed.

WHY TO CHOOSE IT: "Pork butt is a great cut. The upper shoulder has the nicest flavor. It includes some of the most tender cuts in the whole animal because they are less used muscles than those in the lower part of the shoulder, known as the 'pork shoulder,'" says Ronnie.

TWICE-SMOKED PULLED CHICKEN

ACTIVE TIME: 2 HOURS
TOTAL TIME: 23 TO 24 HOURS
SERVES: 10 TO 12

INGREDIENTS

- 20 (6 to 8 ounces, or 170 to 225 g each) bone-in skinless chicken thighs
- 1 batch Chicken Brine (page 23)
- 1 batch Not-So-Basic Chicken BBQ Rub (page 32)
- ½ cup (120 ml) apple juice
- 2 tablespoons (28 ml) water
- ½ cup (112 g) salted butter, cubed
- ¼ cup (85 g) honey
- 2 tablespoons (4 g) chopped fresh thyme leaves
- 2 teaspoons red pepper flakes
- 1 tablespoon (14 g) kosher salt

SPECIAL EQUIPMENT

- Smoker and accessories (see page 212)
- 8-quart (7.6 L) bucket
- Probe thermometer
- Spray bottle
- Fine-mesh strainer

THIS IS WILL'S GRANDFATHER'S RECIPE—SORT OF. HIS GRANDDAD WAS A GREAT COOK, AND WHEN HE PASSED AWAY, HE HANDED DOWN ALL HIS RECIPES TO WILL, INCLUDING HIS FAMOUS LEMON CHICKEN. THAT CHICKEN, COOKED IN BUTTER AND SEASONED WITH THYME, IS STILL A FAVORITE IN WILL'S FAMILY AND THEY'VE ALWAYS WANTED TO SEE IT IN A COOKBOOK. THIS IS WILL'S BBQ VERSION, WHICH GETS ITS BRIGHTNESS FROM APPLE JUICE.

METHOD

Submerge the chicken thighs in the brine in an 8-quart (7.6 L) bucket. Refrigerate for 12 hours.

Prepare your smoker to 275°F (135°C). Have it at this temperature for at least 1 hour before smoke time. (See page 212 for additional information on preparing a smoker.)

Remove the chicken from the brine. Dry each piece with paper towels. When the thighs are very dry, dust each side of each thigh with about 1 tablespoon (10 g) of the rub, shaking off any excess.

Arrange the thighs side by side in your smoker, leaving at least ¼ inch (6 mm) between them. Set your thermometer alarm to 165°F (74°C) and place the probe in the smallest thigh. Put the apple juice in spray bottle and mist the chicken every 20 minutes until it reaches 165°F (74°C), about 1 hour.

While the chicken is smoking, make the butter sauce. Bring 2 tablespoons (28 ml) of water to a boil in a small saucepan over low heat; adjust to a simmer. Add the cubes of butter, one at a time, whisking until melted and fully emulsified before adding the next. Once all the butter is added, whisk in the honey, thyme, red pepper flakes, and salt until the honey is melted. Remove from the heat and keep warm but not hot.

When the thighs reach 165°F (74°C), remove them from the smoker and arrange them in a baking pan large enough to hold all the chicken in a single layer. Pour any remaining apple juice from the spray bottle over the chicken and then drizzle the butter sauce evenly on top. Cover with foil and return to the smoker for 1 hour.

After 1 hour, remove a piece of chicken and test it. It should be soft enough to shred with a fork. If it isn't, smoke for 1 more hour.

Remove the chicken from the baking pan, discard the bones, and shred the meat. Save the liquid to keep the chicken moist. Dust with any remaining chicken rub and serve.

STORAGE

Refrigerate in a tightly sealed container for up to 4 days or freeze for up to 1 month.

CHICKEN BRINE

INGREDIENTS

- 4 quarts (1.8 kg) ice cubes
- 2 quarts (1.9 L) water
- 1 cup (224 g) kosher salt
- 1 cup (200 g) granulated sugar
- 1 crisp tart apple, peeled and quartered
- 1 small yellow onion, peeled and quartered
- 1 tablespoon (5 g) whole black peppercorns, toasted
- 1 tablespoon (6 g) cumin seeds, toasted
- 3 star anise pods, toasted
- 1 bay leaf
- 1 bunch thyme

SPECIAL EQUIPMENT

- 8-quart (7.6 L) bucket
- Fine-mesh strainer

METHOD

Put the ice in an 8-quart (7.6 L) bucket and set aside.

In a large pot, bring the water to a boil. Add the salt, sugar, apple, onion, peppercorns, cumin, star anise, and bay leaf. Stir until the sugar and salt have dissolved. Remove from the heat and add the thyme. Carefully pour the hot liquid over the ice. Stir until the ice fully melts. Allow the brine to sit for 6 hours. Strain the brine, reserving the liquid. Discard the solids.

STORAGE

Store brine in a tightly sealed container at room temperature for up to 1 week.

KINDA SIMPLE BEEF BRISKET

ACTIVE TIME: 30 MINUTES
TOTAL TIME: 16 HOURS
SERVES: 10 TO 12

INGREDIENTS

- 10 to 12 pounds (4.6 to 5.5 kg) packer cut prime beef brisket
- 1¼ cups (188 g) Basic Beef BBQ Rub (see page 32)

SPECIAL EQUIPMENT

- Smoker and accessories (see page 212)
- Pecan and oak or your favorite hardwood
- Probe thermometer
- Neoprene gloves
- Cooler, for holding meat

THIS IS THE LOW-FI VERSION OF A SMOKED BRISKET. IF YOU ARE LOOKING TO WIN A BARBECUE WORLD CHAMPIONSHIP, YOU WANT CHRIS HART'S AMERICAN ROYAL 1ST PLACE BEEF BRISKET RECIPE FROM *WICKED GOOD BBQ*. BUT IF YOU AREN'T QUITE AT THAT LEVEL (YET), THIS SOMEWHAT SIMPLER VERSION IS UNDENIABLY DELICIOUS. ON THE COMPETITION TRAIL OR IN YOUR BACKYARD, THOUGH, THERE'S ONE THING YOU CAN'T COMPROMISE ON: THE QUALITY AND CUT OF THE BEEF. YOU NEED A PACKER CUT PRIME BEEF BRISKET WITH A POINT—THE THINNER EDGE OF THE MEAT—THAT IS AT LEAST 1 INCH (2.5 CM) THICK. MAKE FRIENDS WITH YOUR BUTCHER. THAT'S ONE OF THE REAL SECRETS TO BARBECUE.

METHOD

Preheat your smoker to 250°F (121°C). About 30 minutes before you are ready to cook, stoke the fire with your favorite hardwood; we prefer pecan and oak for this. (See page 212 for additional information on preparing a smoker.)

Pat the brisket dry with paper towels. With a sharp knife, trim off most of the fat from the top, leaving about a ¼ inch (6 mm). Flip over and remove any large pieces of fat and silver skin. Lightly and evenly coat the meat with the rub.

Insert the thermometer probe into the thickest part of the brisket. Place the meat fat-side up in your smoker. Smoke the brisket for about 6 hours, maintaining an ambient temperature of 250°F (121°C). When the internal temperature reaches 160°F to 170°F (71°C to 77°C), it is time to wrap.

To wrap the brisket, place two 2-foot (60 cm) pieces of heavy-duty aluminum foil side by side, overlapping them by 6 inches (15 cm). Take another 2-foot (60 cm) piece of heavy-duty aluminum foil and place it perpendicular across the center of the foil rectangle. With neoprene gloves, carefully take the brisket out of the smoker and remove the probe. Place the brisket in the center of the foil, with the long edge of the brisket parallel to the long edge of the foil. Fold the foil over the brisket and tightly seal all sides.

Place the wrapped brisket back into the smoker. Carefully ease the probe back into the center of the brisket. Continue smoking until the probe reads 202°F (94°C).

CONTINUED

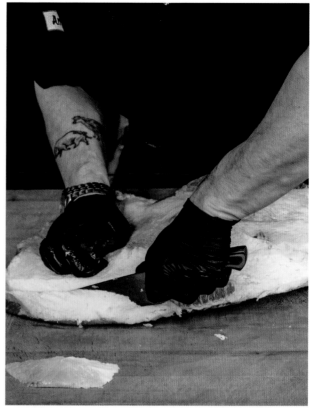

With neoprene gloves, carefully remove the brisket from the smoker and place it on a baking sheet. Open the aluminum foil to let the steam out and let the meat rest for 10 minutes.

If you are going to serve it immediately, let rest for another 10 minutes, and then place the brisket on a cutting board and slice against the grain into ¼-inch (6 mm)-thick slices. There will be juices in the aluminum foil; these are a fantastic addition to BBQ sauce or to use with oysters (page 58).

If you are planning to serve this in a few hours, wrap the brisket in new aluminum foil, repeating the process above. If you are waiting to serve the meat, prepare a tempered cooler by filling the cooler with warm water. Close the lid and wait 10 minutes. Remove the water, place the meat in the warm cooler, and close the lid. You can store the meat for up to 3 hours.

STORAGE

Wrap meat tightly in plastic wrap and refrigerate for up to 4 days or freeze for up to 1 month. Refrigerate brisket juices in a tightly sealed container for up to 3 weeks.

WHAT THE BUTCHER KNOWS:

PACKER CUT BRISKET

WHAT IT IS: The brisket comes from the lower breast of the cow. It is a hardworking muscle that requires proper cooking to tenderize. The packer cut, sometimes called the Texas brisket, is a little different from the traditional flat cut brisket; it also includes the point of the meat, connected to the flat by a thick vein of fat.

WHAT TO ASK FOR: A packer cut, or Texas brisket, is known in the business as NAMP #120. Insist on one that is 1 inch (2.5 cm) thick at its thinnest point.

WHY TO CHOOSE IT: "I love brisket," Ronnie says. "More people ask for single briskets—or the flat cut—but the point piece is really the one that has all the flavor."

NEW MEMPHIS RIBS

ACTIVE TIME: 1 HOUR
TOTAL TIME: 5 TO 5 HOURS
30 MINUTES
SERVES: 8 TO 10

INGREDIENTS

- 6 racks St. Louis–style spareribs, about 3 pounds (1.4 kg) each
- 2 cups (333 g) New Memphis Dry Rub (page 31)
- 1 cup (235 ml) apple juice

SPECIAL EQUIPMENT

- Smoker and accessories (see page 212)
- Probe thermometer
- Spray bottle

CREATING THIS RECIPE FELT LIKE WE WERE REINTERPRETING THE *MONA LISA*. HOW CAN YOU IMPROVE ON A MASTERPIECE? WE STAYED TRUE TO THE TIME-TESTED TECHNIQUE FOR PRODUCING A PERFECT RACK OF MEMPHIS RIBS, BUT WE BROUGHT SOME SMOKE SHOP TRICKS TO THE RUB, ADDING A FEW OF OUR FAVORITE PEPPERS FROM AROUND THE WORLD—ALEPPO, ESPELETTE, GUAJILLO, AND CHILE DE ÀRBOL—TO THE CLASSIC RECIPE.

METHOD

Prepare your smoker to 275°F (135°C). Have it at this temperature for at least 1 hour before smoke time. (See page 212 for additional information on preparing a smoker.)

With a paper towel, peel the membrane off the bone side of the ribs. Dust each rack of ribs evenly with rub, using 1 tablespoon (10 g) on the bone side of each rack and 3 tablespoons (30 g) on the meat side of each rack. Insert the thermometer probe into the meat near the bone at the center of the thinnest rib. Set your thermometer alarm to 192°F (89°C).

Lay the ribs meat-side up in the preheated smoker. Depending on your smoker capacity, the racks may be touching slightly. That's okay. They will shrink. Cover your smoker and set a timer for 1 hour. Put the apple juice in the spray bottle. After 1 hour, spray each rack of ribs twice, pointing the sprayer just above the ribs and not directly at them. Repeat the spray step each hour.

Smoke until the internal temperature is 192°F (89°C), about 3 to 3½ hours. If you pick up a rack in the center with a pair of tongs and the meat is just starting to pull away from the bone, the ribs are done. Let sit for 5 minutes. Liberally dust each rack with 2 tablespoons (20 g) of rub before serving.

STORAGE

Wrap tightly in plastic wrap and refrigerate for up to 4 days or freeze for up to 1 month.

NEW MEMPHIS DRY RUB

ACTIVE TIME: 30 MINUTES
TOTAL TIME: 30 MINUTES
YIELD: 3 CUPS (500 G)

INGREDIENTS

- 1 cup (192 g) turbinado sugar
- ½ cup (100 g) granulated sugar
- ½ cup (112 g) kosher salt
- ½ cup (56 g) paprika
- 2 teaspoons garlic powder
- 2 teaspoons onion powder
- 2 teaspoons porcini powder (see Ingredient Guide, page 217)
- 1 teaspoon Old Bay Seasoning
- 1 teaspoon ground Aleppo pepper (see Ingredient Guide, page 217)
- 1 teaspoon ground Espelette pepper (see Ingredient Guide, page 217)
- 3 or 4 dried guajillo peppers (see Ingredient Guide, page 217)
- 2 dried chile de àrbol, stems removed (see Ingredient Guide, page 217)
- 2 teaspoons cumin seeds

SPECIAL EQUIPMENT

- Spice grinder

METHOD

Preheat the oven to 350°F (180°C, or gas mark 4).

In a medium bowl, combine the turbinado and granulated sugars, salt, and paprika with the garlic, onion, and porcini powders, Old Bay, and Aleppo and Espelette peppers. Whisk thoroughly.

Remove any stems and seeds from the guajillo peppers by cutting off the top and bottom with scissors, and then cutting down one side to open it like a book. Press the guajillos flat on a baking sheet and toast in the oven for 3 to 5 minutes to help release their flavor. When cool enough to handle, break into pieces and grind well in a spice grinder, working in small batches to ensure a fine powder. Add to the spice mix.

Combine the chile de àrbol and cumin seeds in a sauté pan over medium-high heat and toast until fragrant, about 3 minutes. Grind together in a spice grinder and add to the spice mix. Mix again to make sure all the ingredients are incorporated.

STORAGE

Store in a cool, dark place in an airtight container for up to several months.

WHAT THE BUTCHER KNOWS:

ST. LOUIS–CUT RIBS

WHAT IT IS: These are the ribs from the belly side of the pig, trimmed of the cartilage to form a neat rectangle.

WHAT TO ASK FOR: If you want to use the hospitality industry lingo, ask for NAMP #416A.

WHY TO CHOOSE IT: "We have customers who come in saying, 'I want baby backs,' and most of the time I say, 'No, you don't. You want St. Louis–cut ribs.' They have a lot more flavor, they are less expensive, and they have twice the meat. I always recommend them," Ronnie says.

BASIC PORK BBQ RUB

THIS IS A RUB YOU CAN THROW TOGETHER IN JUST A COUPLE OF MINUTES WITH INGREDIENTS FROM YOUR PANTRY. IT'S PERFECT FOR YOUR PORK BARBECUE AND GREAT ON CHICKEN, TOO.

INGREDIENTS

- 4 tablespoons (28 g) paprika
- 2 tablespoons (30 g) packed light brown sugar
- 2 tablespoons (28 g) kosher salt
- 2 tablespoons (26 g) granulated sugar
- 2 tablespoons (15 g) chili powder
- 2 tablespoons (14 g) ground cumin
- 3 tablespoons (18 g) coarsely ground black pepper
- 1 tablespoon (5 g) cayenne pepper

METHOD

Combine all the ingredients in a bowl and mix thoroughly.

STORAGE

Store in a cool, dark place in an airtight container for up to several months.

BASIC BEEF BBQ RUB

HERE'S ANOTHER QUICK RUB RECIPE, THIS ONE HAS A GRATED BOUILLON CUBE FOR ADDITIONAL SAVORINESS. IT'S PERFECT IN RECIPES LIKE OUR KINDA SIMPLE BEEF BRISKET (PAGE 24).

INGREDIENTS

- 1 cup (224 g) kosher salt
- 1 cup (96 g) coarsely ground black pepper
- ½ cup (56 g) onion powder
- ½ cup (72 g) garlic powder
- 1 beef bouillon cube (12 g)

METHOD

Combine the salt, pepper, onion powder, and garlic powder in a bowl. Finely grate the bouillon cube over the bowl of rub. Mix well, making sure there are no lumps remaining.

STORAGE

Store in a cool, dark place in an airtight container for up to several months.

NOT-SO-BASIC CHICKEN BBQ RUB

YOU MIGHT NOT HAVE SZECHUAN PEPPERCORNS IN YOUR PANTRY, BUT THEY ARE WORTH SEEKING OUT FOR THIS PERFECT POULTRY RUB. MAKE A DOUBLE BATCH; IT WILL KEEP FOR MONTHS.

INGREDIENTS

- ½ cup (110 g) turbinado sugar
- ¼ cup (56 g) kosher salt
- ¼ cup (28 g) smoked paprika
- 1 tablespoon (6 g) grated lemon zest
- 1 tablespoon (9 g) garlic powder
- 1 tablespoon (7 g) onion powder
- 1 tablespoon (1 g) dried parsley
- 1 tablespoon (5 g) whole black peppercorns, toasted and ground
- 2 teaspoons Szechuan peppercorns, toasted and ground (see Ingredient Guide, page 217)
- 1 teaspoon red pepper flakes

METHOD

Combine all the ingredients in a medium bowl and mix until thoroughly blended. Be sure to break up any clumps of zest.

STORAGE

Store in a cool, dark place in an airtight container for up to several months.

SMOKY HOT BBQ SAUCE

ACTIVE TIME: 40 MINUTES

TOTAL TIME: 40 MINUTES

YIELD: 3⅓ CUPS (780 ML)

INGREDIENTS

- ½ cup (170 g) blackstrap molasses
- ½ cup (120 ml) apple cider vinegar
- ½ cup (115 g) packed dark brown sugar
- ½ cup (100 g) granulated sugar
- 1 cup (90 g) thinly sliced jalapeño peppers (3 to 4 large jalapeños)
- 2 tablespoons (28 ml) Worcestershire sauce
- 1 tablespoon (16 g) tomato paste
- 1 teaspoon garlic powder
- 1 teaspoon hickory powder (see Ingredient Guide, page 217)
- 1 teaspoon cumin seeds, toasted and ground
- 1 teaspoon yellow mustard seeds
- ½ teaspoon dried thyme
- ½ teaspoon anise or fennel seeds
- 2 cups (480 g) ketchup
- 2 teaspoons kosher salt

THIS IS OUR ODE TO KC MASTERPIECE, THE CLASSIC SUPERMARKET SAUCE EVERYBODY LOVES. YOU NEED A SAUCE LIKE THIS TO STAND UP TO THE BIG BOLD FLAVORS OF BARBECUE. THINK PORK BELLY BURNT ENDS (PAGE 165) OR KINDA SIMPLE BEEF BRISKET (PAGE 24). YES, THERE ARE A LOT OF JALAPEÑOS IN THIS RECIPE, BUT THE HEAT ISN'T OVERWHELMING. (WANT MORE HEAT? USE SOME SERRANO PEPPERS, AKA THE GREEN BULLET FROM HELL.) HICKORY POWDER HELPS BALANCE THE SPICE WITH RICH SMOKINESS. IT'S A BETTER CHOICE THAN LIQUID SMOKE, WHICH CAN BE BITTER.

METHOD

Combine the molasses, vinegar, and brown and granulated sugars in a medium saucepan over medium-high heat and bring to a boil, stirring occasionally. Add the jalapeños, Worcestershire sauce, tomato paste, garlic powder, hickory powder, cumin, mustard, thyme, and anise or fennel seeds. Stir well to incorporate. Reduce the heat and simmer for 5 minutes, stirring occasionally. Whisk in the ketchup and salt and simmer for 2 minutes more.

STORAGE

Cool to room temperature and refrigerate in an airtight container for up to 1 month.

BARE-BONES BBQ SAUCE

ACTIVE TIME: 30 MINUTES
TOTAL TIME: 30 MINUTES
YIELD: 4 TO 5 CUPS (1 TO 1.2 L)

THIS DOWN-AND-DIRTY BARBECUE SAUCE IS AS EASY AS REACHING FOR A JARRED ONE FROM THE SUPERMARKET. CHANCES ARE YOU ALREADY HAVE ALL THE INGREDIENTS IN YOUR PANTRY.

INGREDIENTS

- 1½ cups (300 g) granulated sugar
- 1 cup (225 g) packed light brown sugar
- 1 cup (235 ml) apple cider vinegar
- ½ cup (120 ml) water
- ¼ cup (60 ml) Worcestershire sauce
- 3 tablespoons (33 g) yellow mustard
- 1 tablespoon (9 g) garlic powder
- 1 tablespoon (7 g) ground cumin
- 1 tablespoon plus 2 teaspoons (10 g) coarsely ground black pepper
- 1 tablespoon (5 g) dried thyme
- 2 teaspoons yellow mustard seeds
- 2 teaspoons kosher salt
- 1 teaspoon cayenne pepper
- 2 cups (480 g) ketchup

METHOD

Combine all the ingredients except the ketchup in a medium saucepan over medium-high heat, whisking to blend. Bring to a simmer and cook for 5 minutes, stirring occasionally. Whisk in the ketchup and continue to simmer for 5 minutes more. Remove from the heat.

STORAGE

Cool to room temperature and refrigerate in an airtight container for up to 1 month.

PIT BEANS

INGREDIENTS

- 2 tablespoons (28 ml) vegetable oil
- 1 large white onion, diced (about 2 cups [320 g])
- 2 tablespoons (28 g) kosher salt, divided
- 2½ teaspoons (5 g) coarsely ground black pepper, divided
- 8 ounces (225 g) Kinda Simple Beef Brisket (page 24), cut into ½-inch (1.3 cm) pieces
- ¾ cup (144 g) turbinado sugar or (175 g) packed light brown sugar
- 2 teaspoons red pepper flakes
- 2 cups (480 g) ketchup
- ½ cup (120 ml) apple cider vinegar
- ¼ cup (80 g) blackstrap molasses
- ¼ cup (60 ml) soy sauce
- ¼ cup (60 ml) Frank's RedHot
- 2 tablespoons (22 g) yellow mustard
- 1 cup (235 ml) low-sodium beef broth
- 2 cans (15 ounces, or 425 g each) of Great Northern beans, drained and rinsed
- 2 cans (15 ounces, or 425g each) of pinto beans, drained and rinsed

THE SMOKE SHOP ALWAYS HAD PIT BEANS ON THE MENU, BUT WE DIDN'T NAIL THE DISH UNTIL WILL SHOWED UP. HIS RECIPE CALLS FOR BOTH BROWN SUGAR AND MOLASSES FOR SWEETNESS AND SOY SAUCE AND, OF COURSE, OUR FAVORITE BRISKET (PAGE 24) FOR SAVORINESS. THESE BEANS ARE GREAT FRESHLY MADE, BUT THEY ARE EVEN BETTER A DAY LATER. THE FLAVORS NEED TIME TO MELD. YOU DON'T HEAR THE INDIVIDUAL INSTRUMENTS ANYMORE; YOU HEAR THE WHOLE ORCHESTRA WITH EACH BITE.

METHOD

Preheat the oven to 350°F (180°C, or gas mark 4).

Heat the oil in a large saucepan over medium heat. Add the onion, 2 teaspoons of the salt, and ½ teaspoon of the pepper. Reduce the heat to medium-low and sweat the onions until they are soft and translucent, 10 to 15 minutes. Add the brisket and stir until it is fragrant and the pieces soften and look moist. Stir in the sugar, remaining 2 teaspoons of black pepper, and red pepper flakes and continue cooking until the sugar melts and starts to simmer, about 3 minutes. Use the sugar liquid to scrape up any browned bits from the bottom of the pan.

Increase the heat to medium and add the ketchup, vinegar, molasses, soy sauce, hot sauce, and mustard, stirring to incorporate. Stir in the broth and when the mixture comes to a boil, add the remaining 4 teaspoons (20 g) of salt. Reduce the heat and simmer for 5 minutes, stirring often to prevent the sauce from burning on the bottom. Add all the beans and return to a simmer. Cook for 5 minutes and then cover the pan and place it in the oven to bake for 20 minutes. Remove the cover and bake for another 10 minutes until the surface looks thickened and caramelized. Stir the beans before serving.

STORAGE

Refrigerate in a tightly sealed container for up to 5 days.

BAKED MACARONI & CHEESE WITH BACON AND ASPARAGUS

ACTIVE TIME: 1 HOUR
TOTAL TIME: 1 HOUR 30 MINUTES
SERVES: 12

INGREDIENTS

- 1 package (16 ounces, or 455 g) of ziti
- 12 ounces (340 g) cheddar cheese, grated (about 3 cups [360 g])
- 12 ounces (340 g) Monterey Jack cheese, grated (about 3 cups [345 g])
- 6 ounces (170 g) thick-sliced smoked bacon, diced
- 1 tablespoon (15 ml) vegetable oil
- 1 clove garlic, minced
- 1 bunch asparagus, tough ends trimmed and cut into 1-inch (2.5 cm) pieces
- 10 tablespoons (140 g) unsalted butter, divided
- ½ cup (63 g) all-purpose flour
- 1 teaspoon dried thyme
- 1 teaspoon red pepper flakes
- 6 cups (1.4 L) whole milk
- ½ teaspoon Dijon mustard
- 1½ teaspoons kosher salt
- ½ teaspoon coarsely ground black pepper
- About 30 saltine crackers, crushed

BAKED MAC AND CHEESE HAS TO BE CREAMY AND IT HAS TO BE CRUNCHY. TO GET THE TEXTURE OF THE SAUCE JUST RIGHT, WE USE TWO DIFFERENT CHEESES HERE. YOU NEED THE CHEDDAR FOR THAT CLASSIC FLAVOR, BUT YOU NEED THE MONTEREY JACK, TOO, BECAUSE IT'S A GREAT MELTING CHEESE. FOR THE TOPPING, ANDY INSISTS ON SALTINES. THEY ARE HIS GUILTY PLEASURE. IF YOU WERE A RITZ CRACKER KID, YOU CAN USE THOSE INSTEAD FOR AN EVEN RICHER DISH. THE GOAL IS TO MAKE THIS TASTE LIKE SOMETHING MOM MADE—ONLY BETTER.

METHOD

Preheat the oven to 350°F (180°C, or gas mark 4). Grease the inside of a 3-quart (2.8 L) baking dish.

Bring 8 quarts (7.6 L) of water to a boil in a large pot. Season the water with salt and add the ziti, cooking according to package directions until al dente. Drain the pasta well and transfer to a large bowl.

In another bowl, toss the grated cheeses together.

While the pasta is cooking, combine the bacon, oil, and garlic in a medium heavy-bottomed saucepan over medium-low heat. Cook, stirring occasionally, until the bacon is golden brown and starting to crisp, 8 to 10 minutes. Use a slotted spoon to transfer the bacon to the bowl of ziti, mixing gently to combine. Add the asparagus and 2 cups (235 g) of the cheese mixture and mix again.

Dice 6 tablespoons (85 g) of the butter; you may not use it all. Carefully pour the bacon drippings and garlic into a heatproof glass measuring cup and add enough of the diced butter to make 6 tablespoons (90 g) total fat. Pour it back into the saucepan and melt the butter over low heat. Add the flour, thyme, and red pepper flakes, stirring to coat the flour in the fat, and cook until the mixture starts to look dry, about 5 minutes more.

Gradually add the milk, whisking constantly to be sure there are no lumps, and then whisk in the mustard. Increase the heat to medium and bring the sauce to a simmer, stirring frequently. Reduce the heat as needed to avoid scorching. Once the sauce starts to thicken, continue stirring and cooking for 5 minutes more. Remove the pan from the heat.

Gradually add 3 cups (353 g) of the cheese mixture to the sauce, whisking to melt after each addition. Season the cheese sauce with salt and black pepper to taste and pour it over the ziti, mixing gently to combine.

Transfer to the prepared baking dish, spreading evenly, and scatter the remaining 1 cup (118 g) of cheese over the top.

Melt the remaining 4 tablespoons (55 g) of butter. Combine the melted butter and crushed crackers in a small bowl. Sprinkle evenly over the ziti and bake just until the sauce bubbles around the edges, 15 to 20 minutes. Cool for 10 minutes before serving.

STORAGE

Cover with plastic wrap and refrigerate for up to 4 days.

SMASHED POTATO SALAD

ACTIVE TIME: 1 HOUR

TOTAL TIME: 1 HOUR

SERVES: 10 TO 12

INGREDIENTS

- 2½ pounds (1.1 kg) baby Yukon gold or baby red potatoes
- 2 tablespoons (28 g) plus 1 teaspoon kosher salt, divided
- ¾ cup (175 g) mayonnaise
- 1 tablespoon (11 g) yellow mustard
- 1 tablespoon (9 g) garlic powder
- 1 tablespoon (7 g) onion powder
- 1 tablespoon (15 ml) fish sauce
- 3 scallions, thinly sliced
- 2 stalks celery, diced
- 1 tablespoon (4 g) roughly chopped flat-leaf parsley
- 1 tablespoon (4 g) roughly chopped tarragon leaves
- 1 tablespoon (4 g) roughly chopped dill
- 2 teaspoons fresh lemon juice
- 1 teaspoon coarsely ground black pepper

SURE, YOU COULD MAKE A POLITE POTATO SALAD, WITH PERFECTLY DICED SPUDS. BUT SMASHING THEM IS SO MUCH MORE FUN—AND THE STARCHES IT RELEASES CREATE THE CREAMIEST POTATO SALAD YOU'VE EVER SERVED. (PLUS, IT'S EASIER TO DO WITH SLIGHTLY OVERCOOKED POTATOES, SO YOU DON'T HAVE TO WORRY ABOUT GETTING THE TIMING EXACTLY RIGHT.) THE UNEVEN TEXTURE OF THE SMASHED POTATOES IS BETTER AT CAPTURING THIS UNUSUAL DRESSING. UNLESS YOU ARE A VEGAN, DON'T SKIP THE FISH SAUCE. IT'S A STANDARD IN ANY CHEF'S PANTRY. IT MIGHT SMELL A LITTLE FUNKY STRAIGHT FROM THE BOTTLE, BUT IT'S MAGIC ON THE PLATE.

METHOD

Place the potatoes in a large pot and cover with 4 quarts (3.8 L) of cold water. Bring to a boil over high heat, add 2 tablespoons (28 g) of the salt, and cook until the potatoes are tender and slightly overcooked, 20 to 30 minutes; they will be easy to pierce with a knife. Drain and let cool.

When the potatoes are cool enough to handle, use a large spoon to smash them, one at a time, on a sheet pan. There should be large chunks and small bits. Cool to room temperature.

Whisk the mayonnaise, mustard, garlic powder, and onion powder in a large bowl to blend. Add the fish sauce and mix well and then add the scallions, celery, parsley, tarragon, and dill and mix again. Fold in the cooled potatoes and season with the lemon juice, the remaining 1 teaspoon of salt, and the pepper. Serve at room temperature.

STORAGE

Cover with plastic wrap and refrigerate for up to 1 day.

ACTIVE TIME: 40 MINUTES

TOTAL TIME: 2 HOURS

SERVES: 10 TO 12

MAC SALAD

FOR WILL, A BARBECUE ISN'T COMPLETE WITHOUT MACARONI SALAD. THE BEST ONES COMBINE THE CRUNCH OF RAW VEGETABLES WITH SOFT PASTA. WILL SUGGESTS COOKING YOUR MACARONI FOR A LITTLE LONGER THAN USUAL TO GIVE IT A MORE TENDER TEXTURE. KEWPIE MAYONNAISE, A JAPANESE CONDIMENT THAT IS SMOOTHER THAN ITS AMERICAN COUNTERPART, ISN'T STANDARD AT A SOUTHERN POTLUCK, BUT THE CREAMINESS AND RICHNESS IT PROVIDES WILL MAKE YOUR DISH A STANDOUT.

INGREDIENTS

- 2 tablespoons (28 g) plus 1 teaspoon kosher salt, divided
- 1 pound (455 g) elbow macaroni
- 2 tablespoons (28 ml) vegetable oil
- ½ small red bell pepper, diced
- ½ small green bell pepper, diced
- ¼ small red onion, diced
- 1 stalk celery, diced
- 1 scallion, thinly sliced
- 1 teaspoon chopped tarragon leaves
- 1 teaspoon chopped flat-leaf parsley
- ½ teaspoon coarsely ground black pepper
- ½ teaspoon garlic powder
- 1 cup (225 g) Kewpie mayonnaise (see ingredient Guide, page 217)
- 2 teaspoons yellow mustard
- 3 hard-boiled eggs, chopped

METHOD

Bring 4 quarts (3.8 L) of water to a boil in a large pot. Season the water with 2 tablespoons (28 g) of the salt and add the macaroni, cooking according to package directions plus 1 minute, stirring often. The pasta should be a little past al dente. Drain the pasta well, toss it with the oil, and spread it out on a sheet pan to cool to room temperature.

While the pasta is cooling, combine the red and green peppers, onion, celery, and scallion in a large bowl. Add the tarragon, parsley, remaining 1 teaspoon of salt, pepper, and garlic powder; toss to blend.

In a separate bowl, stir the mayonnaise and mustard together and then fold in the hard-boiled eggs. Scrape this mixture into the vegetables and mix well. Fold in the cooled macaroni and chill for 1 hour before serving.

STORAGE

Refrigerate in a tightly sealed container for up to 4 days.

SWEET 'N' SPICY COLESLAW

ACTIVE TIME: 35 MINUTES
TOTAL TIME: 45 MINUTES
SERVES: 10 TO 12

INGREDIENTS

- 1½ cups (340 g) mayonnaise
- ¼ cup (60 g) prepared horseradish
- 3 tablespoons (42 g) kosher salt
- 3 tablespoons (36 g) sugar
- 2 teaspoons garlic powder
- 2 teaspoons ground ginger
- 2 teaspoons celery seeds
- 1 teaspoon cayenne pepper
- 1 teaspoon coarsely ground black pepper
- 2 teaspoons Tabasco Original Red Sauce
- 1 teaspoon Frank's RedHot
- 8 cups (720 g) minced green cabbage (1 medium head cabbage)
- 2 cups (220 g) peeled and minced carrots (3 to 4 medium carrots)

SPECIAL EQUIPMENT

- Food processor

THERE ARE SOME INGREDIENTS IN THIS RECIPE YOU MAY NEVER HAVE CONSIDERED ADDING TO COLESLAW BEFORE. THE GROUND GINGER AND THE HORSERADISH DON'T ANNOUNCE THEMSELVES LOUDLY, BUT IF YOU FORGOT THEM, YOU'D KNOW SOMETHING WAS MISSING. SOMETHING ELSE YOU DON'T WANT TO LEAVE OUT: THE FOOD PROCESSOR. YOU CAN MINCE THE CABBAGE AND CARROTS BY HAND, BUT IT WILL TAKE FOREVER. CUT THE CABBAGE INTO NARROW WEDGES AND USE THE CHEESE GRATER ATTACHMENT ON YOUR FOOD PROCESSOR TO MAKE QUICK WORK OF IT.

METHOD

Whisk the mayonnaise, horseradish, salt, sugar, garlic powder, ginger, celery seeds, cayenne pepper, and black pepper together in a small bowl. Let the dressing sit for about 10 minutes to allow the flavors to bloom. Whisk in the two hot sauces.

Toss the cabbage and carrots together in a large bowl. Add 1 cup (221 g) of the dressing and toss until well coated. Cover and refrigerate until serving time. Just before serving, toss the slaw with the rest of the dressing.

STORAGE

Refrigerate in a tightly sealed container for up to 3 days.

the SmokeShop
by Andy Husbands

CHARRED CAYENNE LEMONADE WITH A KICK

🕐 **ACTIVE TIME:** 30 MINUTES
TOTAL TIME: 5 HOURS 30 MINUTES
SERVES: 10

INGREDIENTS

- 10 lemons
- 2½ cups (450 g) sugar
- ⅛ teaspoon cayenne pepper
- 8 cups (1.9 L) warm water
- 2½ cups (570 ml) Deep Eddy Sweet Tea vodka
- Ice cubes

SPECIAL EQUIPMENT

- Fine-mesh strainer

THIS IS AN ARNOLD PALMER, BBQ STYLE. CARAMELIZING THE LEMONS GIVES THE JUICE A SMOKY FLAVOR, AND DEEP EDDY SWEET TEA VODKA, MADE IN TEXAS, IS THE BEST WE'VE EVER TASTED. MICHAEL BOUGHTON CAME UP WITH THIS RECIPE AND THE TRICK WITH THE FROZEN LEMON RINDS. THEY ENHANCE THE FLAVOR OF YOUR DRINK, MAKE IT LOOK NICE, AND KEEP IT COLD WITHOUT WATERING EVERYTHING DOWN. BRILLIANT.

METHOD

Preheat a cast-iron pan over high heat until smoking.

Cut the lemons in half crosswise and dip the cut sides in sugar. Place the lemons sugar-side down on the heated pan and let caramelize until dark brown, 5 to 7 minutes. Be careful not to burn them. Remove from the pan and let cool.

Juice the grilled lemon halves. Freeze the spent lemon rinds for at least 5 hours or overnight. Strain the lemon juice into a gallon (3.8 L) pitcher with a cover. Add the rest of the sugar, cayenne pepper, and warm water to the pitcher and stir until the sugar is dissolved.

Add the vodka to the lemonade ½ cup (120 ml) at a time; stir and taste after each addition until it is to your liking.

Cover and refrigerate the lemonade until cool.

Before serving, place the frozen lemon halves into the pitcher to keep the lemonade cool. Pour into small glasses over ice.

KENNY'S BUTTER CAKE AND THE CRACK

ACTIVE TIME: 20 MINUTES
TOTAL TIME: 1 HOUR 20 MINUTES
SERVES: 12

INGREDIENTS

- ¼ cup (50 g) granulated sugar
- ½ cup (112 g) unsalted butter, at room temperature
- 4 large eggs, divided
- 1 box of pound cake mix (16 ounces, or 455 g)
- 3¾ cups (450 g) confectioners' sugar
- 8 ounces (225 g) cream cheese, at room temperature

SPECIAL EQUIPMENT

- Stand mixer

KENNY GOODMAN GAVE US THIS RECIPE, WHICH IS ALSO KNOWN AS ST. LOUIS OOEY GOOEY CAKE. HE'S THE PHOTOGRAPHER WHO TOOK THE AWESOME PHOTO OF THE CAKE YOU SEE HERE (AND ALL THE OTHER DELICIOUS IMAGES IN THE BOOK). KENNY AND ANDY ARE ON THE SAME COMPETITION BARBECUE TEAM, IQUE, AND THIS CAKE HAS WON HIM MANY AWARDS. WHEN WE STARTED SERVING IT AT THE RESTAURANT, WE TRIMMED OFF THE EDGES TO MAKE EVERY PIECE THE SAME. WE WOULD JUST SNACK ON LEFTOVERS IN THE KITCHEN. THAT'S WHERE THEY GOT THE NAME "THE CRACK." THOSE SCRAPS ARE ADDICTIVE—AND WE DECIDED WE NEEDED TO SHARE.

METHOD

Preheat the oven to 350°F (180°C, or gas mark 4). Generously grease a 9 × 13-inch (23 × 33 cm) baking pan. Dust the baking pan with the granulated sugar, making sure the interior is completely coated. Discard any remaining sugar.

In the bowl of a stand mixer fitted with a paddle attachment, beat the butter, 2 of the eggs, and the cake mix until combined. Using a plastic spatula, spread the batter into the prepared pan and smooth to create an even surface.

In the bowl of a stand mixer fitted with a paddle attachment, beat the confectioners' sugar, cream cheese, and remaining 2 eggs until smooth. With a plastic spatula, spread the mixture evenly over the cake batter.

Place the pan in the oven and bake until the top is golden and pillowy, about 40 minutes. To test for doneness, insert a toothpick into the center. It will come out covered in the cream cheese mixture, but without any cake clinging to it.

Transfer to a wire rack and let cool for at least 20 minutes.

Once cool, cut ½-inch (1.3 cm) off each side of the cake. This is The Crack and it is the very best part. Cut the remaining cake into 12 even pieces.

STORAGE

Cover the cake with plastic wrap and refrigerate for up to 5 days. The Crack won't keep; you'll eat it all yourself!

THE COCKTAIL
PARTY

SAY THE WORDS "COCKTAIL PARTY" AND PEOPLE PICTURE *SEX IN THE CITY*. AND WE DO HAVE A PRETTY PINK DRINK FOR YOU—A CLASSIC BROWN DERBY DOLLED UP WITH POMEGRANATE TEA (PAGE 71). SEE, OUR SMOKY VERSION OF A COCKTAIL PARTY IS A LITTLE MORE FUN THAN YOUR TYPICAL HIGH HEELS AND BOW-TIE AFFAIR. HERE, YOU CAN NIBBLE ON OYSTERS ON THE HALF SHELL (PAGE 58) *AND* PIGS IN A BLANKET (PAGE 60).

There are two secrets to throwing a great cocktail party: popcorn and math. No, really. People come to a cocktail party hungry, so you want to have something for them to snack on when they walk through the door. At our soirees, that's popcorn— sometimes with Creole spices (page 68) and sometimes with honey and lime zest (page 70). We serve it in a big crystal bowl, and we put the bowl as far away from the kitchen as possible. You want to give people someplace else to hang out while you are putting the finishing touches on the Clams Casino, BBQ Style (page 63).

Once your party is off to a great start, the worst possible thing—besides running out of booze, of course—would be running out of food. That's where the math comes in. We've figured out that, on average, one person mingling at a cocktail party eats about 24 ounces (680 g) of food in an hour and a half. That's 10 to 12 of the small bites in this chapter. From there, you just have to multiply—and always keep the punch bowl full.

CITY HAM AND EGGS

ACTIVE TIME: 1 HOUR 30 MINUTES

TOTAL TIME: 1 HOUR 30 MINUTES

SERVES: 10 TO 12 (24 PIECES)

INGREDIENTS

- 2 tablespoons (28 ml) vegetable oil, divided
- 2 dozen quail eggs
- Kosher salt and coarsely ground pepper, as needed
- ½ cup (120 g) Herb Butter (page 54), at room temperature
- 6 square slices white bread
- 2 tablespoons (8 g) finely chopped parsley
- 2 tablespoons (8 g) finely chopped tarragon
- ¼ cup (44 to 60 g) your favorite mustard
- 1 pound (455 g) City Ham 2.0 (page 53), sliced as thinly as possible

IN ANDY'S LAST BOOK, *PITMASTER*, YOU'LL FIND A RECIPE FOR CITY HAM. THAT RECIPE IS DELICIOUS—BUT THAT DIDN'T STOP US FROM TRYING TO MAKE THE HAM EVEN BETTER WITH THE ADDITION OF HERBS AND SOME UNEXPECTED SPICES. HERE, WE PAIR OUR NEW VERSION WITH A BRUNCH CLASSIC, BUT YOU'LL ALSO HAVE PLENTY OF LEFTOVER HAM TO USE ANYWAY YOU SEE FIT.

METHOD

Preheat the oven to 250°F (125°C, or gas mark ½).

Preheat a cast-iron pan or griddle over medium heat. Use a paper towel to coat the pan with 1 tablespoon (15 ml) of the oil. One at a time, use a paring knife to slice off the pointed end of each quail shell, pour the egg into a small bowl, and carefully pour it into the pan. Season with salt and pepper and cook for 2 to 3 minutes until the white is set but the yolk is still runny. Slide a spatula (a small offset spatula is best) under the eggs to loosen and transfer them to a sheet pan as they are done. Work in batches, using the remaining 1 table-spoon (15 ml) of oil as needed to avoid crowding. Wipe the pan and place it back over medium-high heat to grill the toast.

For the toast, spread about 1 tablespoon (15 g) of Herb Butter on one side of the bread and cook for about 3 minutes, butter-side down, until golden brown. Turn and cook the second side until toasted, about 1 minute more.

Combine the parsley and tarragon in a small bowl.

Spread 1 slice of toast with about 2 teaspoons of mustard and place it on a cutting board. Arrange 3 or 4 thin ham slices (about 2 ounces [55 g]) on top, overlapping if necessary, to cover the toast without going over the edges. Use a large knife to cut straight down through the ham and bread to form 2 triangles. Repeat in the other direction for a total of 4 triangles. Transfer the toast points to a sheet pan and repeat with the remaining ham and toast. Sprinkle some herbs on top of each toast point and center a fried egg on each one.

Place the sheet pan in the oven for 3 to 5 minutes to heat through without cooking the egg yolks. Arrange on a platter and serve immediately.

STORAGE

Store the toast in a tightly sealed container for up to 1 day. Refrigerate the fried quail eggs on a sheet pan covered tightly in plastic wrap for up to 1 day.

CITY HAM 2.0

ACTIVE TIME: 45 MINUTES
TOTAL TIME: 4 HOURS 15
MINUTES PLUS 6 DAYS
YIELD: 3 POUNDS (1.4 KG)

INGREDIENTS

- 4 cups (946 ml) water
- 3 quarts (1.4 kg) ice cubes
- 2 dried guajillo peppers (see Ingredient Guide, page 217)
- 3 star anise pods
- 3 tablespoons plus 1 teaspoon (17 g) whole coriander seeds
- 2 tablespoons (10 g) whole black peppercorns
- ⅔ cup (133 g) sugar
- ½ cup (112 g) kosher salt
- ⅓ cup (18 g) dried rosemary leaves
- ⅓ cup (14 g) dried thyme
- 2 teaspoons red pepper flakes
- 1 bay leaf
- 4 teaspoons (24 g) Prague powder #1, also known as pink curing salt
- 3 pounds (1.4 kg) center-cut pork loin

SPECIAL EQUIPMENT

- 8-quart (7.6 L) bucket
- Smoker and accessories (see page 212)
- Hickory or your favorite hardwood
- Probe thermometer

METHOD

In a medium saucepan over high heat, bring the water to a boil. While the water heats, put the ice in the bucket, which will be your brining container.

In a large sauté pan over medium-high heat, toast the guajillos, star anise, coriander, and black peppercorns until fragrant and starting to color, 2 to 3 minutes.

When the water boils, turn off the heat. Add the sugar and salt, stirring until both are dissolved. Stir in the toasted spices, rosemary, thyme, red pepper flakes, and bay leaf. Pour the water over the ice and stir until the ice is melted. Add the Prague powder to the cold liquid and stir to incorporate. Refrigerate the brine for 12 hours.

Submerge the pork loin in the chilled brine, cover it tightly, and refrigerate for 5 days.

Preheat your smoker to 245°F (118°C). About 30 minutes before you are ready to cook, stoke the fire with your favorite hardwood; we prefer hickory for this. (See page 212 for additional information on preparing a smoker.)

Remove the ham from the brine and pat it dry with paper towels. Place the ham fat-side up in your smoker with a thermometer probe in the center and cook until it reaches 155°F (68°C), 2 to 2½ hours. Remove the ham from the smoker and let it rest on a cutting board for 30 minutes before slicing.

STORAGE

Wrap tightly in plastic wrap and refrigerate for up to 4 days or freeze for up to 1 month.

HERB BUTTER

ACTIVE TIME: 10 MINUTES
TOTAL TIME: 10 MINUTES
YIELD: ABOUT ½ CUP (120 G)

INGREDIENTS

- ½ cup (112 g) unsalted butter, softened
- 1 tablespoon (4 g) finely chopped parsley
- 1 teaspoon finely chopped tarragon
- 1 teaspoon garlic powder
- ½ teaspoon onion powder
- ½ teaspoon coarsely ground black pepper

SPECIAL EQUIPMENT

- Electric mixer

METHOD

Combine all the ingredients in a mixing bowl. Use an electric mixer to whip until smooth.

STORAGE

Refrigerate in a tightly sealed container for up to 1 month.

WHAT THE BUTCHER KNOWS:

PORK LOIN

WHAT IT IS: It is a cut from the pig's back. (Pork loin is completely different from pork tenderloin; don't get confused.)

WHAT TO ASK FOR: You want a boneless, center-cut pork loin, known as NAMP #413A.

WHY TO CHOOSE IT: It's ideal for smoking at low temperatures and grilling at high temperatures.

PORK BELLY PASTRAMI SKEWERS

ACTIVE TIME: 1 HOUR 15 MINUTES
TOTAL TIME: 2 DAYS
SERVES: 10 TO 12 (16 TO 18 PIECES)

INGREDIENTS

- 12 cups (2.8 L) water
- ¾ cup (168 g) kosher salt
- ½ cup (100 g) sugar
- 5 tablespoons (30 g) pickling spice
- 1 tablespoon (18 g) Prague powder #1, also known as pink curing salt
- 1½ teaspoons dried rosemary leaves
- 1½ teaspoons garlic powder
- 1½ teaspoons whole black peppercorns
- 2 pounds (900 g) boneless, skinless pork belly, frozen for 2 hours before cutting
- 1 batch Pastrami Rub (page 57)
- Beer Mustard (page 57), for serving

SPECIAL EQUIPMENT

- 1-gallon (3.8 L) container
- Smoker and accessories (see page 212)
- Pecan or your favorite hardwood
- 16 to 18 (12-inch [30 cm]) long, thin wooden skewers

PASTRAMI IS NOT SOMETHING PEOPLE MAKE AT HOME VERY OFTEN. THEY SHOULD. IT DOES TAKE A COUPLE OF DAYS TO PREPARE, BUT MOST OF THE PREP WORK IS AT THE BEGINNING OF THE PROCESS, WHICH MAKES IT PERFECT FOR A PARTY. ON THE DAY OF THE BASH, YOU JUST HAVE TO LIGHT UP YOUR SMOKER AND DUST THE SKEWERS WITH THE RUB. WE'VE MADE OUR PASTRAMI WITH JUICY PORK BELLY, NOT THE USUAL BRISKET, BUT IT IS JUST AS GOOD WITH MUSTARD AS THE CLASSIC IS. YOU CAN USE A BASIC DIJON OR OUR VERSION, SWEET AND HOPPY WITH CARAMELIZED ONIONS AND BEER.

METHOD

Combine the water, salt, sugar, pickling spice, Prague powder, rosemary, garlic powder, and peppercorns in a large saucepan and bring to a boil over medium-high heat, stirring continually to dissolve the salts and sugar. Remove from the heat and cool to room temperature. Refrigerate for 24 hours.

Cut the semi-frozen pork belly against the grain into sixteen to eighteen 6-inch (15 cm)-long, ¼-inch (6 mm)-thick strips. With the back of a wooden spoon, lightly pound the meat a few times to make it thinner, about ⅛ inch (3 mm) thick. Place the strips in a 1-gallon (3.8 L) container and pour the brine over them. Make sure all the meat is submerged. Refrigerate, covered, for 12 hours.

Preheat your smoker to 275°F (135°C). About 30 minutes before you are ready to cook, stoke the fire with your favorite hardwood; we prefer pecan for this. (See page 212 for additional information on preparing a smoker.)

While the smoker is heating, remove the meat from the brine, swishing off any pickling spice stuck to the strips. Pat them as dry as possible with paper towel. Push a skewer through the length of each pork belly strip, leaving about 1½ inches (3.8 cm) of skewer showing at the top for easier serving and eating. Dust each side with the rub. Place the skewers ½ inch (1.3 cm) apart in the smoker. (If possible, remove the smoker rack to arrange the skewers.) Cook for 1 hour.

To serve, stand the skewers in a beer glass or Mason jar. Serve with the Beer Mustard for dipping.

STORAGE

Wrap tightly in plastic wrap and refrigerate for up to 4 day or freeze for up to 1 month.

PASTRAMI RUB

ACTIVE TIME: 5 MINUTES
TOTAL TIME: 5 MINUTES
YIELD: ABOUT 1 CUP (113 G)

INGREDIENTS

- 8 tablespoons (40 g) coarsely ground coriander seeds
- 7 tablespoons (42 g) coarsely ground black pepper
- 3 tablespoons (21 g) paprika
- 2 teaspoons kosher salt

METHOD

Combine all the ingredients in a bowl and mix thoroughly.

STORAGE

Store in a cool, dark place in an airtight container for up to several months.

BEER MUSTARD

ACTIVE TIME: 15 MINUTES
TOTAL TIME: 15 MINUTES
YIELD: 1 CUP (235 ML)

INGREDIENTS

- 1 tablespoon (15 ml) olive oil
- 1 cup (80 g) thinly sliced red onion (½ small red onion)
- ¼ teaspoon kosher salt
- 1 cup (235 ml) hoppy beer, such as a New England–style double IPA
- ¼ cup (60 g) packed light brown sugar
- 2 tablespoons (28 ml) apple cider vinegar
- ¼ teaspoon ground allspice
- ½ cup (120 g) French's Stone Ground Dijon Mustard

METHOD

Heat the oil in a small saucepan over medium-high heat. Add the onion and salt and cook, stirring continually until softened and browned, about 5 minutes. Add the beer, brown sugar, vinegar, and allspice, stirring to combine. Reduce the heat and simmer until the liquid has reduced to a syrup just thick enough to coat the onions, about 5 minutes more. Cool for 10 minutes and then fold in the mustard until evenly mixed.

STORAGE

Cool to room temperature and refrigerate in an airtight container for up to 1 month.

WHAT THE BUTCHER KNOWS:

PORK BELLY

WHAT IT IS: It is a fatty slab from the belly of the pig, popular in many cuisines around the world.

WHAT TO ASK FOR: In butcher speak, you want NAMP #409B, the boneless, skinless belly. The same advice applies to the belly as to any cut from the pig: buy from a reputable supplier and ask for a heritage breed, which will have better flavor.

WHY TO CHOOSE IT: "Anything pork belly is a score for me," says Ronnie, who finds the cut very versatile. He likes to slice pork belly like bacon and fry it up in a pan with a little oil and salt. "The best fresh bacon in the world."

OYSTERS ON THE HALF SHELL

ACTIVE TIME: 2 HOURS
TOTAL TIME: 3 HOURS 30 MINUTES
PLUS 1 DAY
SERVES: 10 TO 12 (36 PIECES)

SMOKE WORKS MAGIC ON OYSTERS, LOOSENING THE SHELLS (NO DANGEROUS SHUCKING!) AND GIVING THE MEAT A UNIQUE TEXTURE SOMEWHERE BETWEEN A RAW OYSTER AND A COOKED ONE. A TIP FROM THE RESTAURANT: THE BEST WAY TO SERVE OYSTERS IS TO DUMP A COUPLE CUPS OF KOSHER SALT ON YOUR SERVING TRAY AND NESTLE THE SHELLS SECURELY IN THE SALT. FEELING ESPECIALLY FANCY? ADD SOME WHOLE BLACK PEPPERCORNS TO THE DISPLAY FOR COLOR.

INGREDIENTS

- 2 large shallots, minced (about ½ cup [80 g])
- ¼ cup (60 ml) Kikkoman mirin rice wine
- ¼ cup (60 ml) Marukan rice wine vinegar
- 2 teaspoons whole black peppercorns, toasted and coarsely ground
- ¼ teaspoon granulated sugar
- ⅛ teaspoon kombu dashi powder (see Ingredient Guide, page 217)
- 36 oysters
- 2 tablespoons (28 ml) brisket juices (see Kinda Simple Beef Brisket, page 24) or Worcestershire sauce
- 1 small bunch fresh dill, for garnish

SPECIAL EQUIPMENT

- Coarse scrub brush
- Smoker and accessories (see page 212)
- Oyster knife
- Cheesecloth or coffee filter

METHOD

Combine the shallots, mirin, rice wine vinegar, toasted pepper, sugar, and dashi powder in a small bowl. The longer the mignonette sauce sits, the better it gets. For best results, make it at least 1 day in advance. Store it in a tightly sealed container in the refrigerator.

When ready to cook, wash the oysters under cold water, scrubbing to remove any dirt or sand. Discard any oysters with open shells, as this is a sign that they are dead.

Preheat your smoker to 300°F (150°C). (See page 212 for additional information on preparing a smoker.) Place your oysters on the smoker rack. (If possible, remove the smoker rack to arrange the oysters.) Place a baking pan under the rack to catch the oyster liquor. Smoke the oysters for 30 minutes without peeking and then transfer them to the pan with the oyster liquor and set aside at room temperature to cool.

When the oysters are cool enough to handle, use the oyster knife to prepare them. Holding the oyster over the pan to reserve any remaining juices, pry off the flat top shell. Carefully release the meat by scraping the knife along the inside of the top shell. Discard the top shell and any stray bits of debris. Place all the loosened oysters in their bottom shells on a serving tray.

Strain the oyster liquor through cheesecloth or a coffee filter and drizzle a small amount over each oyster. Vigorously whisk the brisket juices into the mignonette and spoon roughly ½ teaspoon over each oyster. (You will not use all the mignonette. The leftovers make a great vinaigrette. Just measure out 3 parts mignonette to 1 part extra virgin olive oil and whisk.) Garnish each oyster with a small sprig of fresh dill and serve immediately.

STORAGE

Refrigerate the mignonette in a tightly sealed container for up to 1 week.

PIGS IN A BLANKET

EVERYBODY WHO'S EVER THROWN A KIDS' PARTY KNOWS HOW TO MAKE PIGS IN A BLANKET: POP OPEN A CAN OF READY-MADE CROISSANT DOUGH. BUT FOR OUR COCKTAIL SOIREE WE PUT A LITTLE LIPSTICK ON THESE PIGS. THE QUICK PUFF PASTRY IS A FLAKY, AIRY, AND BUTTERY VERSION OF CANNED DOUGH, MADE MORE DECADENT WITH HEAVY CREAM AND PARMESAN CHEESE.

INGREDIENTS

- 1 batch Quick Puff Pastry (page 62)
- 1 large egg
- 2½ teaspoons (9 g) yellow mustard
- 8 all-beef hot dogs
- ½ cup (120 ml) heavy cream
- ½ cup (40 g) shredded Parmesan cheese
- 2 tablespoons (30 g) ketchup, for garnish

SPECIAL EQUIPMENT

- Parchment paper
- Pastry brush

METHOD

Line a sheet pan with parchment paper.

On a lightly floured work surface, roll the puff pastry into a ¼-inch (6 mm)-thick, 11 × 16-inch (28 × 40 cm) rectangle. Cut in half lengthwise and then cut each half into 4 equal pieces to make eight 4 by 5½-inch (10 by 14 cm) strips.

Whisk together the egg and mustard to make an egg wash. Brush 1 pastry rectangle with egg wash and place 1 hot dog along a long edge; the pastry and hot dog should be just about the same length. Roll up the hot dog snugly in the pastry, pinching the seam and ends closed. Place the wrapped hot dog on the parchment-lined sheet pan, seam-side down. Repeat with the remaining hot dogs and dough. Refrigerate until firm and cold, about 20 minutes.

Preheat the oven to 375°F (190°C, or gas mark 5).

Remove the wrapped hot dogs from the refrigerator. Brush each generously with the heavy cream and sprinkle each with about 1 tablespoon (5 g) of shredded Parmesan cheese. Bake until golden brown, 10 to 15 minutes. Let cool on the pan for 10 minutes.

Transfer to a cutting board and use a serrated knife to cut each hot dog into 4 or 5 pieces. Arrange on a serving platter and top each piece with a generous dab of ketchup. Serve immediately.

STORAGE

The pastry-wrapped hot dogs can be frozen, tightly wrapped individually in plastic wrap, for up to 1 month. Defrost for several hours before baking.

QUICK PUFF PASTRY

ACTIVE TIME: 30 MINUTES
TOTAL TIME: 1 HOUR 40 MINUTES
YIELD: ABOUT 1½ POUNDS (680 G)

INGREDIENTS

- 1 cup (225 g) unsalted butter, cut into ½-inch (1.3 cm) cubes
- 2 cups (240 g) bread flour
- ¼ cup (31 g) all-purpose flour
- 1 teaspoon kosher salt
- About ⅔ cup (160 ml) cold water, as needed

SPECIAL EQUIPMENT

- Food processor

METHOD

Place the butter cubes on a plate in the freezer for 30 minutes. Meanwhile, combine the bread flour, all-purpose flour, and salt in a food processor.

Scatter the frozen butter over the flour and process in five 2-second pulses; the butter should still be in chunks, distributed throughout the flour. Transfer the contents of the food processor to a medium bowl. Make a well in the flour and add ½ cup (120 ml) of the water, mixing gently until you have a firm dough. Add more water as needed. Depending on the weather and age of your flour, you may not need all the water or you may need to add up to 1 tablespoon (15 ml) more. Gently gather the dough into a ball and wrap it in plastic wrap. Flatten into a disk and refrigerate for 20 minutes.

Knead the dough gently on a lightly floured work surface for about 4 minutes; the dough will become smoother and more uniform as you knead, with large streaks of butter throughout the dough. Form into a smooth rectangle and roll the dough into a 10 × 20-inch (25 × 51 cm) rectangle. Keep the edges as straight and even as possible. The dough should still look marbled with butter.

Fold the dough in thirds, as if folding a piece of paper to put in an envelope. Give the dough a quarter turn and roll out again until about 30 inches (76 cm) long. Repeat the folding step, cover with plastic wrap, and chill for at least 20 minutes before using.

STORAGE

Refrigerate the dough, wrapped in plastic wrap, for up to 5 days; freeze for up to 1 month.

CLAMS CASINO, BBQ STYLE

ACTIVE TIME: 1 HOUR 15 MINUTES
TOTAL TIME: 1 HOUR 45 MINUTES
SERVES: 10 TO 12 (36 PIECES)

THIS IS THE KIND OF RECIPE WE LOVE: A FANCY CLASSIC THAT WE CAN GIVE A FUN BARBECUE TWIST. THE BRINY FRESHNESS OF CLAMS IS A PERFECT PAIRING FOR THE SMOKE. PLUS, WE'RE ALWAYS COOKING TOO MUCH BRISKET. THIS IS A FANTASTIC WAY TO USE SOME OF THE LEFTOVERS.

INGREDIENTS

- 36 littleneck clams, washed to remove any sand
- 4 ounces (115 g) Kinda Simple Beef Brisket (page 24), chilled and trimmed of fat
- 2¼ cups (225 g) crumbled cornbread or 2¼ cups (115 g) panko breadcrumbs
- 3 tablespoons (42 g) unsalted butter, softened
- 3 tablespoons (3 g) roughly chopped cilantro
- 2¼ teaspoons Basic Beef BBQ Rub (page 32)
- Kosher salt and coarsely ground black pepper, to taste
- 1 batch Clam Butter (page 65)

SPECIAL EQUIPMENT

- Smoker and accessories (see page 212)
- Pecan, oak, or your favorite hardwood
- Coarse scrub brush
- Food processor
- Fine-mesh strainer
- Cheesecloth or coffee filter

METHOD

Preheat your smoker to 300°F (150°C). (See page 212 for additional information on preparing a smoker.) About 30 minutes before you are ready to cook, stoke the fire with your favorite hardwood; we prefer pecan or oak for this.

While the smoker is heating, wash the clams under cold water, scrubbing to remove any sand and discarding any with open shells, as this is a sign that they are dead. Place the clams on the smoker rack. (If possible, remove the smoker rack to arrange the clams.) Place a baking pan under the rack to catch the juices. Smoke the clams for 30 minutes without peeking; they should all be popped wide open. Remove them from the smoker and transfer to the baking pan.

Line a baking sheet with aluminum foil and set it aside. Line a fine-mesh strainer with cheesecloth or a coffee filter and set it over a bowl.

Place the brisket in a food processor and pulse until coarsely and evenly minced. Add the cornbread crumbs, butter, cilantro, and BBQ rub. Pulse until evenly combined. Season to taste with salt and pepper, cover, and refrigerate until needed.

When the clams are cool enough to handle, pry each one open over the baking pan and discard the empty shell. Use a paring knife to free each clam from its shell, taking care to remove any bits of debris. Return the loose meat back to the shell and place it on the baking sheet. Strain the liquid in the baking pan through the lined strainer, discarding the solids. Reserve the liquid for the Clam Butter (page 65).

Use a knife or an offset spatula to cover each clam with about 2 teaspoons of the Clam Butter, and then gently press about 1 tablespoon (15 g) of crumbs on top. Cover and refrigerate until party time.

To serve, bring the tray of clams to room temperature. Preheat the oven to 375°F (190°C, or gas mark 5) and bake the clams until the crumbs are golden brown and the butter is bubbling, 15 to 20 minutes. Let the clams cool for 5 minutes before serving with tiny cocktail forks.

STORAGE

Refrigerate unbaked clams for up to 1 day.

CLAM BUTTER

ACTIVE TIME: 30 MINUTES
TOTAL TIME: 1 HOUR 15 MINUTES
YIELD: ABOUT 1½ CUPS (432 G)

INGREDIENTS

- ⅔ cup (150 g) unsalted butter, softened, divided
- ½ small yellow onion, minced (about ⅓ cup [55 g])
- 2 cloves garlic, minced
- Clam drippings from Clams Casino, BBQ Style (see page 63)
- 1 medium carrot, peeled and diced (about ⅓ cup [43 g])
- 2½ tablespoons (40 ml) dill pickle juice
- 2½ tablespoons (40 ml) white wine or water
- 1 lemon, zested and juiced
- 4 teaspoons (20 ml) Bare-Bones BBQ Sauce (page 35)
- 1 teaspoon Old Bay Seasoning
- ¼ teaspoon red pepper flakes
- 2 ounces (55 g) Kinda Simple Beef Brisket (page 35), chilled and trimmed of fat
- 3 tablespoons (12 g) roughly chopped dill
- 1 large dill pickle spear, diced
- Kosher salt and coarsely ground black pepper, to taste

SPECIAL EQUIPMENT

- Food processor
- Electric mixer

METHOD

Heat 1 tablespoon (14 g) of the butter in a medium saucepan over medium heat. Add the onion and cook, stirring continually, until softened and starting to color, about 5 minutes. Add the garlic and cook for 30 seconds more. Add the clam drippings. Add the carrot, pickle juice, wine, lemon zest and juice, BBQ sauce, garlic, Old Bay, and red pepper flakes and bring to a boil over medium-high heat. Lower the heat to a simmer and reduce the sauce until most of the liquid has evaporated and the onions are jammy, 15 to 20 minutes. Remove from the heat and cool to room temperature.

Place the brisket in a food processor and pulse until coarsely and evenly minced.

Place the remaining softened butter in a medium bowl. Add the brisket, dill, diced pickle, and cooled onion mixture and mix with an electric mixer. Season carefully to taste with salt and black pepper; it may not need much at all.

STORAGE

Refrigerate in a tightly sealed container for up to 2 days.

BBQ PEANUTS

INGREDIENTS

- ½ cup (60 g) confectioners' sugar
- 7 tablespoons (66 g) Basic Pork BBQ Rub (page 32) or your favorite rub
- ¼ cup (24 g) chipotle powder
- 1 tablespoon (12 to 13 g) turbinado or granulated sugar
- 2 teaspoons Old Bay Seasoning
- 1 teaspoon kosher salt
- ¼ teaspoon hickory powder (optional; see Ingredient Guide, page 217)
- 4½ cups (655 g) unsalted dry-roasted peanuts
- 1 egg white, lightly beaten

SPECIAL EQUIPMENT

- Silicone baking mat or parchment paper

THIS IS ONE OF THOSE "OH, WOW" RECIPES. PEOPLE DON'T USUALLY EXPECT MUCH OUT OF A BOWL OF BAR NUTS, AND THEN THEY TRY THESE ONES, AND SAY, "OH, WOW." THEY ARE INTOXICATINGLY GOOD—SWEET AND SALTY, SPICY AND SMOKY—AND PEOPLE CANNOT STOP EATING THEM. WE MIX THIS RECIPE UP SOMETIMES BY ADDING DIFFERENT NUTS, FOR A TOTAL OF 4½ CUPS (655 G). YOU CAN USE WALNUTS, PECANS, PEPITAS, SUNFLOWER SEEDS, WHATEVER YOU LIKE. JUST DON'T EXPECT THERE TO BE ANY LEFTOVERS.

METHOD

Preheat the oven to 325°F (170°C, or gas mark 3).

Line a baking sheet with a silicone baking mat or parchment paper. Set aside.

Mix together the confectioners' sugar, rub, chipotle powder, turbinado sugar, Old Bay, salt, and hickory powder, if using, in a small bowl. In a large bowl, combine the peanuts and egg white, mixing until the peanuts are evenly coated. Add the spice mixture to the peanuts and mix again until evenly coated.

Spread the peanuts in a single layer on the prepared pan and bake for 10 minutes. Stir well and bake for 10 minutes more until the peanuts have a nice crust. They will still look slightly tacky. Set the pan on a wire rack for at least 10 minutes. The nuts will get crunchier as they cool.

STORAGE

Store at room temperature in an airtight container for up to 2 weeks.

CREOLE POPCORN

ACTIVE TIME: 45 MINUTES
TOTAL TIME: 1 HOUR
SERVES: 10 TO 12

INGREDIENTS

- 2 tablespoons (28 ml) vegetable oil
- ½ cup (107 g) mushroom popcorn kernels (see Ingredient Guide, page 217)
- 3 tablespoons (18 g) Creole Spice (page 69)
- 1 tablespoon (14 g) kosher salt
- 1 teaspoon baking soda
- ¾ cup (170 g) packed light brown sugar
- 6 tablespoons (85 g) unsalted butter
- 3 tablespoons (45 ml) light corn syrup

PEOPLE WHO THINK CARAMEL CORN ONLY COMES IN A TIN ARE ALWAYS IMPRESSED BY THIS SWEET-AND-SAVORY BAR SNACK INVENTED BY PASTRY CHEF KATE HOLOWCHIK. YOU DON'T HAVE TO TELL ANYONE HOW EASY IT IS TO MAKE. YOU CAN USE THE TYPICAL "MICKEY MOUSE" POPCORN (THINK ABOUT THE SHAPE OF THE POPPED CORN—IT HAS EARS!), BUT THE MUSHROOM-SHAPED POPCORN YOU FIND IN CRACKER JACK DOESN'T BREAK AS EASILY, HOLDS THE SPICED CARAMEL BETTER, AND JUST LOOKS NICER.

METHOD

Preheat the oven to 400°F (200°C, or gas mark 6).

Heat the oil in a heavy-bottomed, medium saucepan with a lid over medium-high heat until you can see streaks in the oil. Add the corn kernels, cover the pan, and continually shake the pan back and forth over the heat until the corn has thoroughly popped, about 2 minutes. Quickly pour it into a large, deep-sided roasting pan and remove any unpopped kernels. (You can also use air-popped popcorn, if you prefer.)

Combine the Creole Spice, salt, and baking soda in a small bowl.

Combine the brown sugar, butter, and corn syrup in a small saucepan over medium heat. Bring to a boil and cook for 3 minutes, stirring continually; the mixture will look puffy and begin to pull away from the pan as you stir. Remove from the heat and quickly stir in the spice mixture. Immediately pour the caramel syrup over the popcorn, stirring gently but quickly to distribute it as evenly as possible before it sets.

Bake the popcorn for 2 minutes. Remove the pan from the oven and gently stir the popcorn to further distribute the softened caramel. Return to the oven and repeat this process 2 or 3 more times until the caramel is evenly distributed; the caramel should still look a bit wet. Do not touch the hot popcorn; it could burn you. Set aside to cool and crisp up.

STORAGE

Store in a cool, dark place in an airtight container for up to 4 days.

CREOLE SPICE

ACTIVE TIME: 5 MINUTES
TOTAL TIME: 5 MINUTES
YIELD: ½ CUP (48 G)

INGREDIENTS

- 2 tablespoons (8 g) dried thyme
- 2 tablespoons (4 g) dried basil
- 2 tablespoons (14 g) paprika
- 1 tablespoon (9 g) garlic powder
- 1 tablespoon (5 g) cayenne pepper
- 2 teaspoons coarsely ground black pepper
- 1 teaspoon chili powder

METHOD

Combine all the ingredients in a bowl and mix thoroughly.

STORAGE

Store in a cool, dark place in an airtight container for up to several months.

HONEY–ALEPPO PEPPER POPCORN

ACTIVE TIME: 45 MINUTES
TOTAL TIME: 1 HOUR
SERVES: 10 TO 12

PIT MASTER TUFFY STONE USES ALEPPO PEPPER IN HIS BARBECUE RUBS. IT HAS A DEEP CHILE FLAVOR WITHOUT OVERWHELMING HEAT AND A SLIGHT HINT OF FLORAL CITRUS. WE DECIDED IT WOULD TASTE GREAT ON POPCORN AMPED UP WITH HONEY AND LIME ZEST. WE WERE RIGHT.

INGREDIENTS

- 2 tablespoons (28 ml) vegetable oil
- ½ cup (107 g) mushroom popcorn kernels (see Ingredient Guide, page 217)
- 3 tablespoons (15 g) ground Aleppo pepper (see Ingredient Guide, page 217)
- 2 tablespoons (28 g) kosher salt
- 1½ teaspoons baking soda
- 1 teaspoon cayenne pepper
- ¾ teaspoon dried rosemary
- ¾ cup (170 g) packed light brown sugar
- 6 tablespoons (120 g) honey
- 6 tablespoons (85 g) unsalted butter
- Grated zest from 4 limes (about 8 teaspoons [16 g])

METHOD

Preheat the oven to 325°F (170°C, or gas mark 3).

Heat the oil in a heavy-bottomed, medium saucepan with a lid over medium-high heat until you can see streaks in the oil. Add the corn kernels, cover the pan, and continually shake the pan back and forth over the heat until the corn has thoroughly popped, about 2 minutes. Quickly pour it into a large, deep-sided roasting pan and remove any unpopped kernels. (You can also use air-popped popcorn, if you prefer.)

Combine the Aleppo pepper, salt, baking soda, cayenne pepper, and rosemary in a small bowl.

Combine the brown sugar, honey, butter, and lime zest in a small saucepan over medium heat. Bring to a boil and cook for 3 minutes, stirring continually; the mixture will look puffy and begin to pull away from the pan as you stir. Remove from the heat and quickly stir in the spice mixture. Immediately pour the caramel syrup over the popcorn, stirring gently but quickly to distribute it as evenly as possible before it sets.

Bake the popcorn for 5 minutes. Remove the pan from the oven; gently stir the popcorn to further distribute the softened caramel. Return to the oven and repeat this process 2 or 3 more times until the caramel is evenly distributed and any uncoated spots are just starting to color. Do not touch the hot popcorn; it could burn you. Cool for 15 to 20 minutes.

STORAGE

Store in a cool, dark place in an airtight container for up to 4 days.

ACTIVE TIME: 20 MINUTES

TOTAL TIME: 1 HOUR PLUS OVERNIGHT

SERVES: 8 TO 10

DOWNTOWN DERBY

THIS IS A PARTY-FRIENDLY VERSION OF THE BROWN DERBY, A DELICIOUS CLASSIC COCKTAIL WITH BOURBON, GRAPEFRUIT, AND HONEY. TO TURN IT INTO A MAKE-IN-ADVANCE PUNCH, MICHAEL ADDED PINK POMEGRANATE TEA. MIX UP EVERYTHING EXCEPT THE WINE A COUPLE OF DAYS BEFORE YOUR BASH TO LET THE FLAVORS MELD. ADD THE BUBBLES JUST BEFORE EVERYONE ARRIVES TO MAKE THE DRINK SPARKLE.

INGREDIENTS

- 3 large grapefruits, divided
- 1 pomegranate
- 3 cups (700 ml) water, divided
- 4 pomegranate-green tea bags
- 1 cup (340 g) honey
- 3 cups (700 ml) bourbon
- 1 cup (235 ml) sparkling wine

SPECIAL EQUIPMENT

- Fine-mesh strainer

METHOD

To cut 1 grapefruit into 1-inch (2.5 cm) wedges, halve the grapefruit through the stem end, quarter each half in the same direction, and then quarter each piece crosswise. Cut the pomegranate in half through the stem end. Freeze the pomegranate and grapefruit pieces separately overnight.

To make the pomegranate tea, heat 2 cups (475 ml) of the water in a small saucepan over medium-high heat until almost boiling. Remove from the heat and add the tea bags; steep for 10 minutes. Discard the tea bags and set the tea aside to cool.

Remove the zest from the remaining 2 grapefruits with a grater. Halve each grapefruit through its equator and juice. Strain the juice through a fine-mesh strainer into a bowl. You should have about 1½ cups (355 ml) of juice. Add the cooled tea and refrigerate while you prepare the rest of the punch.

Stir the grated zest, honey, and remaining 1 cup (235 ml) water in a bowl until the honey dissolves. Let stand for 20 minutes. Stir again, and then strain through the fine-mesh strainer, reserving the liquid and discarding the zest.

To serve, combine the chilled juice mixture, grapefruit-honey syrup, and bourbon in a punch bowl; stir to blend. Add the frozen grapefruit wedges and pomegranate halves and top with the sparkling wine. Ladle into small punch cups.

COCONUT COLD BREW MARTINI

ACTIVE TIME: 5 MINUTES
TOTAL TIME: 20 MINUTES
SERVES: 1

INGREDIENTS

- 1 cup (235 ml) refrigerated unsweetened coconut milk
- 1 cup (200 g) sugar
- ¼ cup (15 g) coconut shavings
- 1½ tablespoons (25 ml) dark rum
- 1½ tablespoons (25 ml) Rum Haven coconut rum
- 2 tablespoons (28 ml) cold brew coffee
- Ice cubes
- 3 whole coffee beans, for garnish

SPECIAL EQUIPMENT

- Cocktail shaker

THIS IS A SOPHISTICATED LITTLE SIPPER THAT PACKS A LOT OF FLAVOR INTO JUST 4 OUNCES (120 ML). THE COCONUT IS THE KEY. WE USE A COCONUT RUM THAT IS LESS SWEET AND HIGHER PROOF THAN MOST OF THE USUAL SUSPECTS AND REFRIGERATED COCONUT MILK—NOT CANNED COCONUT MILK, AN ENTIRELY DIFFERENT PRODUCT—TO GIVE THE DRINK ITS DISTINCTIVE CREAMINESS.

METHOD

To make coconut milk syrup, whisk the coconut milk and sugar in a bowl until the sugar is completely dissolved. This will make more syrup than needed for 1 drink. Refrigerate extra syrup for up to 2 weeks.

Preheat the oven to 350°F (180°C, or gas mark 4). Spread a thin layer of coconut on a baking sheet. Bake for 2 to 3 minutes until the shavings are lightly toasted. Set aside to cool.

Combine the dark rum, coconut rum, cold brew coffee, and 1 tablespoon (15 ml) of coconut milk syrup in a cocktail shaker. Add ice cubes. Shake for 10 to 15 seconds and strain into a martini glass. Garnish with a pinch of toasted coconut shavings and the whole coffee beans.

CHEESECAKE BITES

ACTIVE TIME: 40 MINUTES

TOTAL TIME: 2 HOURS

SERVES: 10 TO 12 (24 PIECES)

INGREDIENTS

- 18 Nilla Wafer cookies
- 4½ tablespoons (59 g) sugar, divided
- 2½ tablespoons (35 g) unsalted butter, melted and cooled
- 7 ounces (200 g) cream cheese, at room temperature
- 1 large egg
- 2 tablespoons (28 ml) heavy cream
- 2 tablespoons (30 g) sour cream
- ½ teaspoon cornstarch
- ½ teaspoon vanilla extract
- Pinch of ground nutmeg

SPECIAL EQUIPMENT

- Mini-muffin pan with 24 cups
- 24 mini-muffin pan liners
- Food processor
- Electric mixer

THIS CHEESECAKE RECIPE STARTED AS A MISTAKE. SARAH WAS RUSHING. SHE WAS DISTRACTED BY THE KIDS AND THE DOG AND SHE THREW ALL THE INGREDIENTS FOR THE FILLING INTO THE BOWL AT ONE TIME AND TURNED ON THE MIXER. IT SHOULD HAVE BEEN A CHEESECAKE DISASTER, BUT INSTEAD IT TURNED INTO ONE OF THE EASIEST AND MOST DELICIOUS SHE HAS EVER MADE.

METHOD

Preheat the oven to 375°F (190°C, or gas mark 5). Line the pan with the muffin pan liners. Place the cookies in a food processor and pulse to fine crumbs. Transfer to a small bowl. Add 1½ tablespoons (20 g) of the sugar and stir to blend. Add the melted butter and stir until evenly mixed; it should have the consistency of wet sand. Divide the crumbs among the cups, using 1 rounded teaspoon per cup. Use the rounded back of a measuring spoon or your fingers to press the crumb crusts in place. Bake for 4 minutes.

While the crusts bake, mix the cheese filling. In a bowl, beat the cream cheese with an electric mixer until smooth and fluffy. Add the remaining 3 tablespoons (39 g) of sugar, the egg, cream, sour cream, cornstarch, vanilla, and nutmeg. Beat at medium speed just to incorporate; scrape down the sides and the bottom of the bowl. Beat again at medium speed until the batter has some small lumps and looks runny, about 1 minute more.

When the crusts are ready, divide the filling among them using about 1 tablespoon (15 g) to fill each one nearly to the top. Return the pan to the oven and bake until the tops are golden, 30 to 35 minutes, rotating the pan after 15 minutes to avoid any oven hot spots. Turn off the oven and leave the pan inside with the door slightly ajar for 10 minutes more.

Cool the cheesecakes in the pan for 30 minutes and then chill the room temperature cakes for at least 15 minutes before serving. Serve chilled or allow to return to room temperature.

STORAGE

Refrigerate in a tightly sealed container for up to 4–5 days.

RED VELVET CAKE

ACTIVE TIME: 30 MINUTES
TOTAL TIME: 1 HOUR
SERVES: 10 TO 12 (24 PIECES)

SARAH NAILED THE TEXTURE OF THIS CAKE. IT IS VELVETY SOFT, AS THE NAME PROMISES. AND HER SOUR CREAM FROSTING IS THE PERFECT FOIL FOR THE RICH CHOCOLATE. A TIP FROM SARAH: IF YOU ARE GETTING CRUMBS IN YOUR FROSTING WHEN YOU CUT THIS, USE UNFLAVORED DENTAL FLOSS INSTEAD OF A KNIFE. REALLY. ELEVATE THE CAKE SLIGHTLY AND PULL A LENGTH OF FLOSS DOWN THROUGH THE CAKE, ALL THE WAY TO THE BOTTOM. SLIDE THE FLOSS OUT AT THE BOTTOM AND REPEAT.

INGREDIENTS

- 1½ cups (180 g) cake flour
- 1½ cups (300 g) sugar
- ¼ cup (20 g) Dutch-processed cocoa powder
- 1½ teaspoons baking soda
- 1½ teaspoons baking powder
- ½ teaspoon kosher salt
- 2 large eggs
- ¾ cup (180 g) sour cream
- ¾ cup (175 ml) warm water
- 2 tablespoons (28 g) unsalted butter, melted and cooled
- 2 tablespoons (28 ml) vegetable oil
- ¾ teaspoon vanilla extract
- ½ teaspoon white vinegar
- 1 tablespoon (15 ml) red liquid food coloring
- 1 batch Sour Cream Frosting (page 77)

SPECIAL EQUIPMENT

- 18 × 13-inch (46 × 33 cm) sheet pan with ¾-inch (1 cm)-high sides
- Parchment paper
- Stand mixer

METHOD

Preheat the oven to 350°F (180°C, or gas mark 4). Line the sheet pan with parchment paper. Grease and flour the paper and sides of the pan.

Combine the cake flour, sugar, cocoa, baking soda, baking powder, and salt in the bowl of a stand mixer fitted with a paddle attachment. Give the ingredients a quick stir to mix together. Then, add the eggs, sour cream, water, butter, oil, vanilla, vinegar, and food coloring. Mix everything together on medium speed for about 2 minutes, stopping at least once to scrape down the bowl. Pour the batter into the prepared pan.

Bake for 25 to 30 minutes until the top of the cake springs back when pressed lightly and a toothpick inserted into the center comes out clean. Cool in the pan on a wire rack for 10 minutes. Turn out onto the rack to finish cooling.

When the cake is completely cool, cut in half widthwise. Spread half the frosting on one piece of cake. Stack the other piece on top and spread the rest of the frosting on top of that piece of cake. Cut the cake into 1-inch (2.5 cm) squares. While cutting, wipe the knife blade off after each cut to keep from getting crumbs in the top frosting. Let the cake stand, cut, for at least 20 minutes before serving. This allows the frosting to set.

STORAGE

Place some toothpicks into the cake to protect the frosting and then cover with plastic wrap and store at room temperature for 1 day or refrigerate for up to 1 week.

SOUR CREAM FROSTING

ACTIVE TIME: 25 MINUTES
TOTAL TIME: 25 MINUTES
YIELD: ABOUT 3 CUPS (825 G)

INGREDIENTS

- 8 ounces (225 g) cream cheese, at room temperature
- ¾ cup (165 g) unsalted butter, softened
- ¼ cup (60 g) sour cream
- 3 cups (360 g) confectioners' sugar, sifted
- 1 teaspoon vanilla extract

SPECIAL EQUIPMENT

- Stand mixer

METHOD

Cream the cream cheese and butter together in the bowl of a stand mixer fitted with a paddle attachment for about 10 minutes. When the mixture is light, add the sour cream, confectioners' sugar, and vanilla. Beat at a low speed for about 5 minutes. The frosting should be fluffy.

STORAGE

Refrigerate in a tightly sealed container for up to 1 week.

TACO
TUESDAY

TACOS ARE NOT JUST FOR TUESDAYS. THEY ARE A PARTY ANY DAY OF THE WEEK. ANDY AND WILL LEARNED THAT AT AN EARLY AGE. THEY BOTH STILL FONDLY REMEMBER TACO DAYS IN THEIR ELEMENTARY SCHOOL CAFETERIAS.

Everybody, it seems, loves a taco, especially the party host who can prepare the fillings and other fixings in advance and serve everything family style. Tacos are a great way to use leftover barbecue, and it doesn't even matter if people show up a little late; most of these dishes don't have to be served screaming hot. Plus, the guests double as chefs here, creating each bite to their personal specifications. Andy would probably pile Brisket Ropa Vieja onto a tortilla (page 80) and top it with Smoked Salsa (page 88). You should watch him around the Scallion Rice, too (page 92).

Will would fill his plate with BBQ Empanadas (page 84), The Smoke Shop Guac (page 89), and Refried Beans (page 93). The only pressure on the host is to have an ample amount of everything—including hot sauce. If Andy and Will were throwing the party, there'd be Tabasco, Cholula, and sriracha on the table, too.

BRISKET ROPA VIEJA TACOS

ACTIVE TIME: 30 MINUTES
TOTAL TIME: 1 HOUR 30 MINUTES
SERVES: 10 TO 12 (48 PIECES)

WHEN YOU SMOKE A BRISKET, YOU ALWAYS HAVE TOO MUCH FOOD, NO MATTER HOW MANY PEOPLE YOU INVITE. PART OF THE FUN IS COMING UP WITH INTERESTING WAYS TO USE THE LEFTOVERS. SOME OF OUR FAVORITES ARE PIT BEANS (PAGE 37), OYSTERS (PAGE 58), CLAMS (PAGE 63), AND THIS SMOKY, TACO-FIED VERSION OF CUBA'S NATIONAL DISH. SERVE IT WITH SOME SMOKED SALSA (PAGE 88).

INGREDIENTS

- 2 tablespoons (28 ml) olive oil
- 1 large yellow onion, diced
- 4 cloves garlic, minced
- 1 green bell pepper, diced
- 1 red bell pepper, diced
- 1 yellow bell pepper, diced
- 1 jalapeño pepper, cut into ⅛-inch (3 mm) rings with seeds
- 1 tablespoon (8 g) chili powder
- 1 tablespoon (6 g) coarsely ground black pepper
- 2 teaspoons kosher salt, plus more to taste
- 2 teaspoons ground cumin
- 1 teaspoon dried oregano
- ¼ teaspoon ground allspice
- ⅓ cup (80 ml) white vinegar
- 1 can (14.5 ounces, or 411 g) of diced tomatoes with juice
- 1½ cups (355 ml) low-sodium chicken or beef broth
- 1 tablespoon (16 g) tomato paste
- 2½ pounds (1.1 kg) Kinda Simple Beef Brisket (page 24), trimmed of fat and cut into 1-inch (2.5 cm) cubes
- 1 cup (140 g) sliced green olives
- 2 batches Grandma's Tortillas (page 87) or 48 store-bought tortillas

METHOD

Preheat the oven to 350°F (180°C, or gas mark 4).

Heat the oil in a large ovenproof saucepan over medium-high heat and when it is hot, add the onion and garlic. Cook, stirring continually, until the onion starts to color, about 4 minutes. Add the bell peppers and jalapeño; continue to cook until the peppers start to wilt, about 3 minutes. Add the chili powder, black pepper, salt, cumin, oregano, and allspice and cook, stirring, for 30 seconds more.

Add the vinegar and deglaze the pan by scraping the bottom and sides. Add the canned tomatoes, broth, and tomato paste and bring to a simmer, stirring to incorporate. Fold in the brisket, cover, and bake for 1 hour.

Remove from the oven and add the olives, stirring gently to break up some of the beef. Season to taste with salt. Serve with warm tortillas.

STORAGE

Refrigerate in a tightly sealed container for up to 5 days.

PULLED PORK QUESADILLAS

ACTIVE TIME: 1 HOUR
TOTAL TIME: 1 HOUR
SERVES: 10 TO 12 (30 PIECES)

INGREDIENTS

- 1 medium yellow onion, halved lengthwise and sliced as thinly as possible
- 2 red jalapeño peppers, cut into thin rings
- ⅓ cup (80 ml) red wine vinegar
- 2 tablespoons (26 g) sugar
- 1 tablespoon (14 g) kosher salt, divided
- 1 tablespoon (7 g) ground cumin, divided
- 2¼ cups (259 g) shredded Monterey Jack cheese
- 1¼ cups (225 g) crumbled goat cheese
- 1 cup (16 g) roughly chopped cilantro
- 2 teaspoons ground coriander
- 2 teaspoons chili powder
- 2 teaspoons coarsely ground black pepper
- 15 Grandma's Tortillas (page 87) or store-bought tortillas
- 3½ cups (826 g) roughly chopped Classic Pulled Pork (page 18), at room temperature
- 1 cup (230 g) sour cream
- 1 to 2 tablespoons (15 to 28 ml) olive oil

SPECIAL EQUIPMENT

- Fine-mesh strainer

IN A RESTAURANT KITCHEN, NOTHING GOES TO WASTE. THAT PHILOSOPHY LEADS TO SOME PRETTY TASTY INVENTIONS. HERE, WE MAKE QUICK PICKLED JALAPEÑOS AND ONIONS TO GO INSIDE THE QUESADILLA. IT'S CHEESY, SPICY, PORKY HEAVEN. BUT THE GENIUS MOVE IS SAVING THE PICKLING BRINE AND MIXING IT WITH SOUR CREAM FOR DIPPING. WHILE WE'RE GOING OVER THE TOP, SERVE SOME SMOKED SALSA (PAGE 88) AND THE SMOKE SHOP GUAC (PAGE 89), TOO.

METHOD

Place the onion and pepper rings in a shallow bowl. Combine the red wine vinegar, sugar, 1 teaspoon of the salt, and 1 teaspoon of the cumin in a small saucepan over medium-high heat. Bring to a boil, stirring to dissolve the sugar and salt. Remove from the heat and cool for 3 minutes. Pour the vinegar solution over the onions and peppers; let it sit for 5 minutes, give it a stir, and cover and refrigerate until needed.

Combine the Jack cheese, goat cheese, cilantro, coriander, chili powder, black pepper, remaining 2 teaspoons of cumin, and remaining 2 teaspoons of salt in a medium bowl. Toss together lightly to keep the mixture loose and crumbly.

Strain the pickled onions and peppers, reserving both the vegetables and the liquid.

Place the tortillas on your work surface and sprinkle ¼ cup (30 g) of the cheese mixture over each. Spread ¼ cup (30 g) of pulled pork on the bottom half of each tortilla. Top the pork with 2 tablespoons (16 g) of pickled vegetables. Fold the tortillas in half to cover the pickled vegetables, pressing gently to keep it closed.

Combine the sour cream and the pickling liquid, stirring to blend, to make the quesadilla dipping sauce.

Preheat a griddle or cast-iron pan over medium heat. When it is hot, drizzle on the olive oil. Working in batches, add as many quesadillas as will comfortably fit. Cover the quesadillas with a lid or an inverted sheet pan. Cook until light golden brown on one side, about 3 minutes. Carefully flip the quesadillas over and toast the second side, about 3 minutes more. Remove and repeat with the next batch. Cut the quesadillas in half and serve with the sour cream dipping sauce.

STORAGE

Refrigerate the pickled onions and peppers in a tightly sealed container for up to 3 days. Refrigerate the quesadillas in a tightly sealed container for up to 1 week.

BBQ EMPANADAS

🕐 **ACTIVE TIME:** 45 MINUTES
TOTAL TIME: 1 HOUR 45 MINUTES
SERVES: 10 TO 12 (20 PIECES)

ALMOST EVERY CULTURE HAS A TRADITION OF MEAT OR VEGETABLES WRAPPED IN DOUGH. THINK POTSTICKERS, PIEROGI, SAMOSAS, AND, OF COURSE, EMPANADAS. IT SURE DOES MAKE THINGS EASY FOR THE HOST. YOU CAN MAKE THESE IN ADVANCE AND POP THEM IN THE OVEN JUST BEFORE THE GUESTS ARRIVE TO MAKE SURE YOU HAVE SOMETHING HOT TO SERVE THEM WHEN THEY WALK IN THE DOOR.

INGREDIENTS

- 1 cup (125 g) coarsely chopped Twice-Smoked Pulled Chicken (page 21) or other smoked meat
- ¼ cup (28 g) crumbled queso fresco
- ¼ cup (29 g) shredded Monterey Jack cheese
- 2 tablespoons (20 g) minced red onion
- 2 tablespoons (2 g) roughly chopped cilantro leaves
- ½ jalapeño pepper, seeded and minced
- 1 tablespoon (15 ml) Bare-Bones BBQ Sauce (page 35) or your favorite BBQ sauce
- 2 teaspoons white vinegar
- ½ teaspoon ground cumin
- ½ teaspoon ground coriander
- ¼ teaspoon kosher salt
- ¼ teaspoon coarsely ground black pepper
- ¼ teaspoon ground cinnamon
- 1 batch Savory Pie Dough (page 85)
- 1 large egg
- 1 teaspoon water

SPECIAL EQUIPMENT

- 3½-inch (9 cm) round cookie cutter
- Pastry brush
- Parchment paper or silicone baking mat

METHOD

Combine the chicken, cheeses, onion, cilantro, jalapeño, BBQ sauce, vinegar, and spices a bowl and mix together lightly until the ingredients are evenly distributed.

Roll the dough out to ⅛-inch (3 mm) thickness and using a 3½-inch (9 cm) cookie cutter, cut as many circles as possible. Gently reroll the scraps and cut them again, for a total of about 20 rounds. Spread the circles out on a lightly floured surface. Whisk together the egg and water in a small bowl to make an egg wash. Brush the edges of each dough circle with egg wash. Place a scant tablespoon (10 g) of filling in the center of each circle, to within ½ inch (1.3 cm) of the edge. Fold into a half-moon, enclosing the filling. Lightly press around the edge with your fingers to seal and then use a fork to press the seal firmly, without breaking through the dough. Refrigerate the empanadas until cold and firm, 20 to 30 minutes.

Meanwhile, preheat the oven to 350°F (180°C, or gas mark 4). Line a sheet pan with parchment paper or a silicone baking mat.

Place the empanadas at least ½ inch (1.3 cm) apart on the pan. Brush them with egg wash and bake until golden brown, about 30 minutes. Cool for at least 5 minutes before serving.

STORAGE

Refrigerate uncooked empanadas in a tightly sealed container for up to 2 days. Refrigerate leftovers in a tightly sealed container for up to 5 days.

SAVORY PIE DOUGH

ACTIVE TIME: 15 MINUTES
TOTAL TIME: 1 HOUR
YIELD: TWO 9-INCH (23 CM) PIE CRUSTS

INGREDIENTS

- 2 cups (250 g) all-purpose flour, plus more for dusting
- ½ cup (70 g) fine yellow cornmeal
- 2 teaspoons coarsely ground black pepper
- 2 teaspoons dried oregano
- 1 teaspoon garlic powder
- 2 teaspoons kosher salt
- 12 tablespoons (170 g) unsalted butter, chilled and cut into 12 pieces
- 4 tablespoons (50 g) shortening, chilled and cut into 4 pieces
- About ½ cup (120 ml) ice water, divided

SPECIAL EQUIPMENT

- Food processor

METHOD

In a food processor, combine the flour, cornmeal, spices, and salt. Pulse a few times to blend. Scatter the butter and shortening over the flour and pulse in 2-second intervals just until the butter chunks are the size of peas. Transfer the mixture to a large bowl.

Make a well in the center of the flour mixture and add ¼ cup (60 ml) of ice water, tossing with a fork or your fingertips to blend. Add just enough additional water, a little at a time, to evenly moisten the flour and form a smooth dough. To test, pinch a bit of the dough; it should hold together easily but not feel wet or sticky.

Lightly gather the dough into a ball, wrap it in plastic wrap, and flatten it into a disk. Refrigerate until cold and firm, 30 minutes to 1 hour.

STORAGE

Wrap tightly in plastic wrap and refrigerate for up to 2 days.

GRANDMA'S TORTILLAS

ACTIVE TIME: 1 HOUR
TOTAL TIME: 1 HOUR 30 MINUTES
YIELD: 24 PIECES

INGREDIENTS

- 3 cups (375 g) all-purpose flour, plus more for dusting
- 1 cup (106 g) pastry flour
- 1 tablespoon (14 g) kosher salt
- 1 tablespoon (14 g) baking powder
- ½ cup (104 g) lard, chilled (see Ingredient Guide, page 217)
- 1 cup (235 ml) warm water

SPECIAL EQUIPMENT

- Food processor

WILL'S GRANDMA MADE A GREAT TEX-MEX-STYLE FLOUR TORTILLA WITH LARD (OR *MANTECA*, AS IT IS KNOWN IN MEXICO). WILL THINKS THAT IS THE KEY TO THE SILKY TEXTURE AND DISTINCTIVE FLAVOR HE REMEMBERS, BUT YOU COULD USE VEGETABLE SHORTENING IF YOU WANT THESE TO BE VEGETARIAN. EITHER WAY, KEEP THE FAT CHILLED, LIKE YOU WERE MAKING BISCUITS, AND COOK THE TORTILLAS FAST.

METHOD

Combine the all-purpose flour, pastry flour, salt, and baking powder in a food processor. Add the lard in chunks and pulse a few times to distribute. Add the water and blend just until the crumbs start to hold together, about 10 seconds. Transfer to a bowl. If the mixture seems dry, add up to 1 additional tablespoon (15 ml) of warm water. Gather the dough into a ball and transfer to a work surface lightly dusted with flour.

Knead for about 5 minutes to form a smooth, slightly shaggy dough. Cover with a damp towel and let rest for 15 minutes. Divide the dough into 24 equal-size pieces; a kitchen scale can help with consistency. Roll each piece into a smooth ball, cover again with a towel, and let the dough relax for 30 minutes; it will be easier to roll.

Place a griddle or cast-iron pan over medium heat. While it heats, shape the tortillas: place 1 ball of dough on a lightly floured surface. Using a rolling pin, roll it out to a 6½-inch (16.5 cm) circle. To keep the circle even, roll first in a forward to back motion, then side to side, and repeat.

Lay the tortilla on the hot griddle. In 20 to 30 seconds, large bubbles will form on the surface. Use tongs to flip the tortilla and cook just until those bubbles start to toast, about 15 seconds more. Transfer the tortillas to a plate and cover with a dry towel to keep them warm. Repeat with the rest of the dough. Serve warm.

STORAGE

Refrigerate dough in a sealed plastic bag for up to 2 days. Refrigerate tortillas in a sealed plastic bag for up to 7 days.

SMOKED SALSA

INGREDIENTS

- 1 medium yellow onion, halved through the stem end
- 2 tablespoons (28 ml) extra virgin olive oil, plus more as needed
- 2 teaspoons kosher salt, plus more as needed
- 1 lime, juiced (about 2 tablespoons [28 ml])
- 2 cloves garlic, minced
- 1 teaspoon coarsely ground black pepper
- 1 teaspoon red pepper flakes
- 1 serrano pepper, seeded and minced
- ½ cup (8 g) roughly chopped cilantro
- 4 large tomatoes, diced (about 4 cups [720 g])
- ½ small red onion, diced (about ½ cup [80 g])

SPECIAL EQUIPMENT

- Smoker and accessories (see page 212)
- Apple wood, another fruitwood, or your favorite hardwood

WE SMOKE JUST THE ONION HERE, TO GIVE THIS SALSA A LOVELY SMOKINESS, WITHOUT LOSING THE TEXTURE OF FRESH TOMATOES. ANDY RECOMMENDS BUILDING ANY SALSA IN REVERSE: OIL, ACID, SALT, AND SPICES FIRST, AND THEN THE VEGETABLES. THERE'S A METHOD TO HIS MADNESS. THE SPICES INFUSE THE LIQUIDS SO WHEN YOU TOSS EVERYTHING TOGETHER, THE FLAVORS ARE MORE EVENLY DISTRIBUTED.

METHOD

Preheat your smoker to 250°F (121°C). About 30 minutes before you are ready to cook, stoke the fire with your favorite hardwood; we prefer apple wood or another fruitwood for this. (See page 212 for additional information on preparing a smoker.)

Coat the yellow onion halves lightly with a little olive oil and season with salt. Place in the smoker and cook for 30 minutes and then set aside to cool. Dice the onion.

Meanwhile, in a large bowl, combine the 2 tablespoons (28 ml) of olive oil, 2 teaspoons of salt, lime juice, garlic, black pepper, red pepper flakes, serrano pepper, and cilantro. Set aside for 5 minutes.

Add the tomatoes, smoked onion, and red onion and mix well. Season to taste with salt.

STORAGE

Refrigerate for up to 1 day.

THE SMOKE SHOP GUAC

ACTIVE TIME: 25 MINUTES
TOTAL TIME: 30 MINUTES
YIELD: 3 CUPS (700 G)

INGREDIENTS

- 4 Haas avocados
- 1 large lime, juiced (about 3 tablespoons [45 ml])
- 2 tablespoons (20 g) minced red onion
- 2 tablespoons (2 g) roughly chopped cilantro
- ½ jalapeño pepper, seeded and minced (1 tablespoon [6 g])
- 2 cloves garlic, minced
- 1 teaspoon ground cumin
- ½ teaspoon cayenne pepper
- 1 small tomato, diced (about ½ cup [90 g])
- 2 teaspoons kosher salt

YOU HAVE OUR PERMISSION TO EAT THIS GUACAMOLE RIGHT OUT OF THE BOWL. IT'S THAT GOOD. WE AREN'T DOING ANYTHING FANCY HERE. IF YOU CHOOSE PERFECTLY RIPE AVOCADOS AND SEASON THEM WELL, YOU'LL HAVE GREAT GUAC. WE DO HAVE ONE TIP FOR YOU, THOUGH: YOU CAN MAKE THIS IN ADVANCE WITHOUT IT TURNING AN ICKY BROWN. PRESS A PIECE OF PLASTIC WRAP TIGHTLY AGAINST THE SURFACE OF THE GUACAMOLE BEFORE YOU SEAL THE STORAGE CONTAINER AND REFRIGERATE.

METHOD

Halve the avocados and discard the pits. Scoop the flesh into a large bowl, sprinkle on the lime juice, and smash the avocado with a potato masher; be sure to leave plenty of chunks. Add the red onion, cilantro, jalapeño, garlic, cumin, and cayenne pepper, and mix gently to keep the avocado chunky. Let the guacamole sit for 5 minutes and then fold in the tomato and salt.

STORAGE

Press plastic wrap against the surface of the guacamole and refrigerate in a tightly sealed container for up to 1 day.

STREET CORN

ACTIVE TIME: 45 MINUTES
TOTAL TIME: 1 HOUR 45 MINUTES
SERVES: 10 TO 12

INGREDIENTS

- 10 to 12 ears corn, shucked, leaving the stalk attached
- 2 dried guajillo peppers (see Ingredient Guide, page 217)
- 2 tablespoons (10 g) coriander seeds
- 1 teaspoon cumin seeds
- 2 cups (224 g) grated Oaxaca cheese or (240 g) Cotija cheese, divided (see Ingredient Guide, page 217)
- ½ cup (115 g) Kewpie mayonnaise (see Ingredient Guide, page 217)
- ½ cup (112 g) crème fraîche
- 1 tablespoon (15 ml) fresh lemon juice
- 3 cloves garlic, minced
- Kosher salt, to taste
- ¼ cup (4 g) finely chopped cilantro
- ¼ cup (4 g) finely chopped epazote (optional; see Ingredient Guide, page 217)
- 1 lime, cut into quarters

SPECIAL EQUIPMENT

- Smoker and accessories (see page 212)
- Pecan, oak, or your favorite hardwood
- Spice grinder

THE CLASSIC MEXICAN ELOTE, OR STREET CORN, IS CHARRED ON A GRILL BEFORE BEING SLATHERED WITH MAYONNAISE AND ROLLED IN CHEESE. YOU CAN TAKE THAT APPROACH. IT IS AWESOME. BUT WE, OF COURSE, PREFER TO AMP UP THE SMOKINESS. EITHER WAY, DON'T SKIP THE SQUEEZE OF LIME AT THE END.

METHOD

Preheat your smoker to 350°F (180°C). About 30 minutes before you are ready to cook, stoke the fire with hardwood; we prefer pecan or oak. (See page 212 for additional information on preparing a smoker.)

To release the corn silks, soak the shucked ears in cold water for 30 minutes.

While the corn is soaking, remove any stems and seeds from the guajillo peppers by cutting off the stem with scissors and then cutting down one side to open like a book. Combine the guajillos, coriander, and cumin seeds in a small sauté pan over medium-high heat, pressing the guajillos flat. Toast until fragrant and starting to color, about 3 minutes. Let cool. Break the guajillos into pieces and grind with the coriander and cumin in a spice grinder to create a fine powder.

Combine 1½ cups (168 g) of the grated cheese with the mayonnaise, crème fraiche, lemon juice, garlic, and toasted spices in a bowl, mixing until evenly blended. Season to taste with salt. In a separate bowl, mix together the cilantro and epazote, if using.

Remove the corn from the water, shake loose any corn silks, and place in the smoker, as close to the coals as possible. Smoke for 15 minutes.

Remove the corn from the smoker. Working one at a time, coat each ear evenly with the mayonnaise mixture. Arrange the corn on a platter and sprinkle with the remaining ½ cup (56 g) of cheese. Squeeze the lime wedges over the corn and sprinkle with the fresh herb mix.

STORAGE

Any leftover corn can be cut off the cob and refrigerated in a tightly sealed container for up to 4 days.

SCALLION RICE

ACTIVE TIME: 10 MINUTES
TOTAL TIME: 30 MINUTES
SERVES: 10 TO 12

INGREDIENTS

- 1 tablespoon (15 ml) olive oil
- 1 clove garlic, minced
- ½ teaspoon red pepper flakes
- 2 cups (360 g) jasmine rice
- 2 teaspoons ground cumin
- 4 cups (946 ml) boiling water
- 1 bunch scallions, sliced into ⅛-inch (3 mm) rings
- ¼ cup (14 g) finely chopped cilantro
- Kosher salt, plus more to taste

ANDY KNOWS THE SECRET FOR MAKING RICE: A RICE COOKER. IT'S NOT A MUST-HAVE FOR EVERYONE, BUT IT IS A WORKHORSE IN HIS HOME KITCHEN. MADE IN THE RICE COOKER OR ON THE STOVE, THIS SIMPLE CUMIN-SCENTED RICE IS GREAT SERVED ALONGSIDE TACOS. ANDY MADE BRISKET ROPA VIEJA (PAGE 80) WITH THIS SCALLION RICE FOR WILL AND HIS WIFE SARAH WHEN THEIR DAUGHTER WAS BORN.

METHOD

Heat the oil in a medium saucepan over medium-high heat. Add the garlic and red pepper flakes and cook, stirring, until the garlic starts to brown, about 1 minute. Add the rice and cumin and cook, stirring to evenly coat with oil and slightly toast the rice, about 2 minutes more.

Add the boiling water carefully; it will steam and spatter. Bring the mixture to a boil. Partially cover the pan and adjust the heat so the rice simmers for 3 minutes and then give it a good stir to make sure nothing is sticking to the bottom. Replace the lid to partially cover and reduce the heat so the rice simmers until tender, 15 to 17 minutes more.

Transfer the cooked rice to a large bowl and fold in the scallions and cilantro. Season to taste with salt.

STORAGE

Refrigerate in a tightly sealed container for up to 4 days.

REFRIED BEANS

INGREDIENTS

- 2 tablespoons (28 ml) vegetable oil
- 1 large white onion, diced (about 3 cups [480 g])
- 12 cloves garlic, sliced
- 1 tablespoon plus 1½ teaspoons (21 g) kosher salt
- ¼ cup (60 ml) apple cider vinegar
- 2 teaspoons dried oregano
- 2 teaspoons red pepper flakes
- 1 teaspoon ground cumin
- 1 teaspoon ground coriander
- ½ teaspoon coarsely ground black pepper
- 1 cup (235 ml) low-sodium beef broth
- 3 cans (15.5 ounces, or 440 g each) of pinto beans, drained and rinsed
- 4 tablespoons (60 g) tahini
- 2 tablespoons (28 ml) extra virgin olive oil

SPECIAL EQUIPMENT

- Immersion blender

THIS IS A CHEF'S RECIPE. THAT DOESN'T MEAN IT'S COMPLICATED. THAT MEANS IT WAS CREATED AT 3 A.M. AFTER A LONG NIGHT IN THE RESTAURANT KITCHEN AND A FEW AFTER-WORK COCKTAILS. IF THE PARTY ENDED UP AT WILL'S APARTMENT, HE USUALLY MADE TACOS, AND ONE NIGHT, HE SERVED THEM WITH THESE TAHINI-SPIKED REFRIED BEANS. THIS LATE-NIGHT STROKE OF GENIUS WAS INSPIRED BY HIS LOVE OF HUMMUS.

METHOD

Heat the vegetable oil in a medium saucepan over medium heat. Add the onion, garlic, and salt. Reduce the heat to medium-low and cook until the onion is soft and translucent, 10 to 15 minutes. Raise the heat to medium-high and stir in the vinegar; let it reduce by half, about 5 minutes. Add the herbs and spices and cook for 3 minutes, stirring occasionally. Add the broth and bring to a boil. Add the beans, stirring to incorporate. Reduce the heat to a simmer and cook for 5 minutes more. Turn off the heat.

Use an immersion blender to partially puree the mixture. You want it to be chunky. Blend in the tahini and then the olive oil.

Serve warm. If the beans start to thicken up, loosen them up by mixing in ¼ cup (60 ml) of water.

STORAGE

Refrigerate in a tightly sealed container for up to 5 days.

VERDE FRESCA

ACTIVE TIME: 15 MINUTES
TOTAL TIME: 15 MINUTES
SERVES: 1

INGREDIENTS

- 1 cup (200 g) sugar
- ½ cup (120 ml) water
- 1 seedless cucumber, cut into chunks
- 1 serrano pepper, quartered
- 3 sprigs cilantro, divided
- 2 tablespoons (28 g) kosher salt
- ⅛ teaspoon cayenne pepper
- 1 glass bottle (12 ounces, or 355 ml) of lime soda (such as Jarritos or Stewart's Key Lime), ice cold
- 3 tablespoons (45 ml) Blanco Tequila
- 1 lime, juiced (about 1½ tablespoons [25 ml])
- Ice cubes

SPECIAL EQUIPMENT

- Food processor or blender
- Fine-mesh strainer
- Cocktail shaker

BOTTLED COCKTAILS ARE ALL THE RAGE IN RESTAURANTS. THAT'S BECAUSE YOU CAN MAKE THEM AN HOUR IN ADVANCE AND KEEP THEM ON ICE FOR YOUR FIRST GUESTS. THIS SPICY AND FRESH TAKE ON THE CLASSIC PALOMA IS BEST WITH LIME-FLAVORED JARRITOS, A POPULAR MEXICAN SOFT DRINK BRAND.

METHOD

To make the verde syrup, combine the sugar, water, cucumber, serrano pepper, and 2 sprigs of the cilantro in a food processor or blender and puree until the sugar is dissolved, about 1 minute. Strain into a container with a lid, whisking the solids in the strainer to extract all the liquid. Discard the solids and cover the container. This will make more syrup than needed for 1 drink. Refrigerate extra syrup for up to 2 weeks.

In a small bowl, mix the salt and cayenne pepper together.

To make the cocktail, uncap the soda. Make room in the bottle for the rest of the cocktail by pouring one-third of the soda (about ½ cup [120 ml]) into a container for later use. Add the remaining sprig of cilantro to the bottle.

Combine the tequila, 1½ tablespoons (25 ml) of the verde syrup, and the lime juice in a cocktail shaker with ice. Shake vigorously for 10 to 15 seconds and strain it slowly into the soda bottle, stirring gently with a chopstick or skewer. Sprinkle a pinch of cayenne salt on the rim of the bottle.

After mixing a few of these, you can use the reserved soda to make the cocktail in a glass. Use 1 cup (235 ml) of lime soda per drink.

OAXACAN MILK PUNCH

ACTIVE TIME: 15 MINUTES
TOTAL TIME: 3 DAYS
SERVES: 12

MILK PUNCH IS A TRADITIONAL BRANDY TIPPLE FROM THE BRITISH ISLES, CIRCA 1700. FOR TACO TUESDAY, MICHAEL REINVENTED IT ENTIRELY, USING A MEXICAN HORCHATA (A RICE MILK) AND A SMOKY MEZCAL INFUSED WITH THE TROPICAL FLAVOR OF BANANAS. THE ONLY THING HE DIDN'T CHANGE: THE FESTIVE CINNAMON STICK GARNISH.

INGREDIENTS

- 2 bananas
- 1½ cups (355 ml) Del Maguey Vida Mezcal
- 1 batch Homemade Horchata (page 96)
- 1 cup (235 ml) white crème de cacao
- Ice cubes
- Cinnamon sticks or ground cinnamon, for garnish

METHOD

Three days before serving, slice the bananas into a 1-quart (946 ml) container with a tight-fitting lid. Pour the mezcal over them and stir; the banana slices should be fully submerged. Cover and refrigerate for 3 days.

To make the cocktails, use a slotted spoon to remove and discard the bananas from the mezcal; the liquor should be fragrant and slightly syrupy. Combine the horchata, banana-infused mezcal, and crème de cacao in a 2-quart (1.9 L) pitcher and stir to combine. Pour over ice into 12 glasses and garnish with a cinnamon stick.

HOMEMADE HORCHATA

ACTIVE TIME: 15 MINUTES
TOTAL TIME: 1 DAY
YIELD: ABOUT 4 CUPS (960 ML)

INGREDIENTS

- 3 cups (700 ml) water
- ¾ cup (146 g) uncooked white rice, rinsed and drained
- 2 cinnamon sticks (4 inches or 10 cm each)
- 1¼ teaspoon ground cinnamon
- ¾ cup (175 ml) unsweetened almond milk
- 1¼ cup (420 g) agave nectar
- 1 teaspoon vanilla extract

SPECIAL EQUIPMENT

- Blender
- Fine-mesh strainer

METHOD

Combine the water, rice, and cinnamon sticks in a large bowl or container. Cover and refrigerate overnight.

Remove the cinnamon sticks and pour the rice mixture into a blender. Add the ground cinnamon and blend on low speed for 1 to 2 minutes. Strain into a large container and discard the solids. Stir in the almond milk, agave nectar, and vanilla. Cover and refrigerate until needed.

STORAGE

Refrigerate in a tightly sealed container for up to 1 week. Stir well before using.

TRES LECHES MINICAKES

ACTIVE TIME: 40 MINUTES

TOTAL TIME: 1 DAY

SERVES: 10 TO 12 (16 PIECES)

INGREDIENTS

- ¾ cup (165 g) unsalted butter, softened
- 1 cup (200 g) sugar
- 3 large eggs, separated
- ¾ teaspoon vanilla extract
- 1 cup (120 g) cake flour
- ½ teaspoon baking soda
- ½ teaspoon baking powder
- ½ teaspoon kosher salt
- ¾ cup (175 ml) whole milk
- ½ cup (120 ml) sweetened coconut milk
- ½ cup (120 ml) almond milk
- ½ cup (120 ml) heavy cream
- ½ cup (60 g) whipped cream
- Ground cinnamon, for garnish

SPECIAL EQUIPMENT

- Parchment paper
- Stand mixer
- Foil muffin pan liners

LIKE OTHER VERSIONS OF TRES LECHES, THESE MINICAKES ARE SOAKED IN THREE DIFFERENT MILKS. THE SURPRISE IS IN THE CHOICE OF MILKS: ALMOND MILK FOR A LIGHT NUTTINESS, COCONUT MILK FOR A HINT OF SWEETNESS, AND HEAVY CREAM FOR RICHNESS. THE CINNAMON-DUSTED WHIPPED CREAM PILED ON TOP BRINGS THE WHOLE DESSERT TOGETHER.

METHOD

Preheat the oven to 350°F (180°C, or gas mark 4). Grease an 8-inch (20 cm) square baking pan, line the bottom with parchment paper, and grease the parchment. Line a sheet pan with parchment paper.

In the bowl of a stand mixer fitted with a paddle attachment, cream the butter and sugar on medium speed until very light and fluffy, at least 5 minutes. Scrape down the bowl occasionally. Add the egg yolks one at a time, incorporating each yolk fully before adding the next. Add the vanilla and mix.

In a separate bowl, sift together the flour, baking soda, baking powder, and salt. Add one-third of the dry mix to the butter mix and mix. Add half of the whole milk and mix, followed by another third of the dry mix, the remaining whole milk, and the remaining dry mix, mixing the batter between each addition.

In another bowl, whisk the egg whites to stiff peaks. Gently fold them into the batter, incorporating fully. Pour the batter into the prepared pan and smooth the top.

Bake until the top is golden brown and springs back when touched, 28 to 33 minutes. A cake tester inserted into the middle of the cake should come out with a few crumbs. Place the cake pan on a wire rack and allow it to cool for 10 minutes. While

waiting, whisk the coconut milk, almond milk, and heavy cream together in a bowl.

Turn the cake out onto the lined sheet pan. Remove the parchment and flip the cake so the top is facing up. Using a skewer, poke holes all over the top. Slowly pour half the milk mixture over the top of the cake, allowing it to run down the sides. Allow the cake to absorb the milk for 10 to 15 minutes and then poke more holes about 1 inch (2.5 cm) apart and pour about half of the remaining milk mixture over the cake. Let sit at room temperature until the cake is completely cool, about 1½ hours. Cut the cake into 2-inch (5 cm) squares. Pour the rest of the milk mixture over the squares. Cover the cake tightly and refrigerate overnight.

Before serving, bring the cake to room temperature. Place each cake in a muffin pan liner. If there is extra milk mixture on the tray, pour a small amount at the base of each cake. Top with the whipped cream (about half a tablespoon each) and a sprinkle of cinnamon.

STORAGE

The cake without the whipped cream can be refrigerated, tightly covered, for up to 3 days.

MEXICAN CHOCOLATE PANNA COTTA

ACTIVE TIME: 30 MINUTES
TOTAL TIME: 5 HOURS
SERVES: 10 TO 12 (24 PIECES)

ANDY CALLS THIS DESSERT ADULT JELL-O. HE'S RIGHT. IT'S A LOT OF WOBBLY FUN, BUT THE FLAVOR—BASED ON OAXACA'S FAMOUS SPICED HOT CHOCOLATE—IS FAR TOO GOOD TO LEAVE TO THE KIDS.

INGREDIENTS

- ½ cup (120 ml) half-and-half, divided
- 1¼ teaspoons gelatin
- 1¼ cups (295 ml) heavy cream
- 2 tablespoons (26 g) sugar
- Pinch of kosher salt
- ¼ teaspoon ground cinnamon
- ⅛ teaspoon red pepper flakes
- 2 ounces (55 g) bittersweet chocolate, finely chopped
- ½ teaspoon vanilla extract
- ¼ teaspoon almond extract
- Semisweet chocolate shavings, for garnish

SPECIAL EQUIPMENT

- Silicone mini-muffin pan with 24 cups
- Nonstick spray
- Fine-mesh strainer

METHOD

Spray each cup of a silicone mini-muffin tray with nonstick spray. Dab with a paper towel to get even coverage and remove extra spray. Place the tray on a sheet pan.

Pour ¼ cup (60 ml) of the half-and-half into a heatproof bowl. Sprinkle the gelatin over top and let stand until softened, about 12 minutes. Place the bowl in a larger bowl of very hot water and stir until the gelatin has completely dissolved.

Meanwhile, in a saucepan, combine the remaining ¼ cup (60 ml) of half-and-half, heavy cream, sugar, salt, cinnamon, and red pepper flakes. Heat over medium-low heat stirring occasionally, until it just reaches a boil. Remove the pan from the heat, and add the bittersweet chocolate and vanilla and almond extracts, whisking until smooth.

Whisk the gelatin into the chocolate mixture and then pour through a fine-mesh strainer into a container with a spout. Divide the mixture among the muffin cups, filling each one almost to the top. Refrigerate uncovered for 10 to 15 minutes until slightly set and then cover the tray with plastic wrap and refrigerate until set and thoroughly chilled, at least 4 hours or overnight.

To serve, run a spoon round the edge of each cup and then invert the pan and push gently on the bottom of each cup. Sprinkle chocolate shavings over the top. Serve cool or at room temperature.

STORAGE

Refrigerate in the tray and tightly covered for up to 3 days.

THE BIG
BRUNCH

THERE'S SOMETHING SPECIAL ABOUT A BRUNCH. IT'S OFTEN THE ONLY MEAL OF THE WEEK WHERE NO ONE IS IN A HURRY. NO ONE IS RUSHING TO WORK; NO ONE IS RUSHING FROM WORK. THIS—SHARING A MEAL WITH FRIENDS—IS THE ONLY THING ON THE AGENDA.

Coffee and conversation would probably be more than enough to satisfy that impulse to slow down and connect, which is why a brunch is so much fun for the cook. You can do whatever you please: fancy food or casual dishes, tried-and-true recipes or experimental ones, or all the above.

On our brunch buffet you'll always find something savory, like Will's Southern-inspired fried chicken and waffles (page 102), and something sweet, like the Berry Buckle (page 126) recipe that our friend Sarah finally agreed to share. (Andy's been bugging her for years.) Brunch is the only time drinking before noon is encouraged, so of course there's a spicy Bloody Mary (page 122) alongside a nonalcoholic favorite.

But the pièce de résistance is the Biscuit Bar (page 106)—everything you and your guests need to build the perfect breakfast sandwich for a lazy weekend meal.

CHICKEN AND WAFFLES WITH RED EYE GRAVY

ACTIVE TIME: 1 HOUR 45 MINUTES
TOTAL TIME: 2 HOURS 15 MINUTES
PLUS 12-HOUR BRINE
SERVES: 10 TO 12 (16 PIECES)

INGREDIENTS

- 4 cups (946 ml) whole buttermilk
- 1 cup (235 ml) Frank's RedHot
- 5 tablespoons (70 g) kosher salt, divided
- 1 tablespoon (13 g) sugar
- 7 pounds (3.2 kg) chicken, cut into 16 pieces
- 2 cups (256 g) cornstarch
- 2 cups (250 g) all-purpose flour
- 4 tablespoons (55 g) baking powder
- About 6 cups (1.4 L) vegetable oil
- 1 batch Waffles (page 105)
- ½ cup (112 g) unsalted butter, at room temperature
- 1 batch Red Eye Gravy (page 104)
- Fermented Honey Hot Sauce (page 105), for serving
- 2 cups (475 ml) maple syrup, warmed
- Scallions, sliced, for garnish

SPECIAL EQUIPMENT

- 3-gallon (11.4 L) container
- Deep-fry thermometer
- Instant-read thermometer

THERE'S ONE THING WILL WON'T COMPROMISE ON WHEN IT COMES TO THIS RECIPE: IT MUST BE MADE WITH BONE-IN CHICKEN. SURE, THAT MEANS YOU NEED A KNIFE AND FORK, BUT A PROPER PLATE OF CHICKEN AND WAFFLES IS TOO MESSY TO EAT WITH YOUR FINGERS ANYWAY. BONE-IN CHICKEN TASTES MORE LIKE, WELL, CHICKEN, AND THE BONE CONDUCTS HEAT, WHICH ALLOWS THE MEAT TO COOK MORE EVENLY IN THE FRYER.

METHOD

Whisk the buttermilk, hot sauce, 4 tablespoons (56 g) of the salt, and the sugar in a large mixing bowl. Let stand for 2 minutes to dissolve the salt and sugar. Place the chicken in the 3-gallon (11.4 L) brining container and pour the buttermilk mixture over it. Cover and refrigerate for 12 hours.

While the chicken is brining, combine the cornstarch, flour, baking powder, and remaining 1 tablespoon (14 g) of salt in another large bowl and whisk until evenly blended. Store in a tightly sealed container until ready to use.

Take the chicken out of the refrigerator at least 30 minutes before you plan to fry. Attach a deep-fry thermometer to the side of a deep heavy-bottomed pan. Pour the oil in to a depth of 1½ inches (3.8 cm) and place the pan over medium-high heat. Place a wire rack on a sheet pan beside the stove, along with the instant-read thermometer.

While the oil is heating, drain the chicken and discard the brine. When the oil reaches 350°F (180°C), coat the chicken pieces in the flour mixture one at a time and transfer the coated pieces carefully to the hot oil.

Cook in batches to avoid crowding the pan; there should be at least ½ inch (1.3 cm) of space between the pieces. Fry, turning occasionally, until the crust is golden brown and the chicken reaches an internal temperature of 165°F (74°C). Total cooking time should be 10 to 18 minutes per batch, with dark meat cooking more slowly than white. Transfer the pieces to the wire rack to drain as they are done.

Allow the chicken to cool slightly before serving. To serve, divide each waffle into 4 pieces and butter each piece. Place 2 pieces of waffle on each plate and top with 1 piece of chicken. Top with the gravy, hot sauce, and maple syrup and garnish with scallions.

STORAGE

Cool and refrigerate plain fried chicken in a tightly sealed container for up to a week.

RED EYE GRAVY

ACTIVE TIME: 30 MINUTES
TOTAL TIME: 45 MINUTES
YIELD: 4 CUPS (946 ML)

INGREDIENTS

- 4 tablespoons (55 g) unsalted butter
- 1 pound (455 g) City Ham 2.0 (page 53), diced
- ¼ cup (40 g) thinly sliced red onion
- 2 cloves garlic, minced
- 1 teaspoon sugar
- 4 tablespoons (32 g) all-purpose flour
- 2 cups (475 ml) strong coffee
- 2 cups (475 ml) low-sodium chicken broth
- ½ cup (120 ml) half-and-half

METHOD

Melt the butter in a heavy-bottomed, medium saucepan over medium-high heat. As soon as it starts to brown, add the ham and cook, stirring continually, until the ham browns a bit and a crust starts to form in the pan, 4 to 5 minutes. (If the crust starts to burn, lower the heat.) Add the onion and garlic and cook, stirring constantly, just until fragrant, 2 to 3 minutes. Add the sugar, stirring until it dissolves, about 20 seconds and then add the flour. Cook, stirring until no dry flour remains and the mixture smells slightly nutty, about 2 minutes. Add the coffee and scrape up all the brown crust in the bottom of the pan. When the mixture comes to a boil, add the chicken broth and half-and-half. Return to a boil, scraping the bottom of the pan continually, and adjust the heat so the gravy simmers until thickened, about 10 minutes.

STORAGE

Cool to room temperature and refrigerate in a tightly sealed container for up to 5 days.

WAFFLES

ACTIVE TIME: 15 MINUTES
TOTAL TIME: 40 MINUTES
YIELD: 10 OR 11 PIECES

INGREDIENTS

- 4 cups (500 g) all-purpose flour
- ¼ cup (55 g) baking powder
- 1½ tablespoons (21 g) baking soda
- 1 tablespoon (14 g) kosher salt
- 1 tablespoon (13 g) sugar
- 1 teaspoon cayenne pepper
- 5 large eggs
- 3½ cups (820 ml) whole buttermilk
- 1 cup (225 g) unsalted butter, melted
- 2 tablespoons (40 ml) maple syrup

SPECIAL EQUIPMENT

- 7- or 8-inch (18 or 20 cm) waffle iron
- Nonstick spray

METHOD

Sift the flour, baking powder, baking soda, salt, sugar, and cayenne pepper together in a large bowl.

In another bowl, beat the eggs to blend. Add the buttermilk, melted butter, and maple syrup and mix well. Pour over the dry ingredients, stirring until only small lumps remain.

Heat the waffle iron and coat with nonstick spray. Cook the waffles according to the manufacturer's directions, using about ⅔ cup (160 ml) of batter for each waffle. Cook until steam stops coming out of the iron and the waffle is golden brown and crisp, about 4 minutes. Repeat with more nonstick spray and the remaining batter. Cool slightly on a wire rack before serving.

STORAGE

Refrigerate room temperature waffles in a tightly sealed zip bag for up to 24 hours or freeze for up to 2 weeks.

FERMENTED HONEY HOT SAUCE

ACTIVE TIME: 30 MINUTES
TOTAL TIME: 30 MINUTES PLUS 7-DAY FERMENT
YIELD: 3 CUPS (700 ML)

INGREDIENTS

- 1 cup (235 ml) apple cider vinegar
- 25 small cloves garlic
- ⅔ cup (230 g) honey
- 12 to 18 Fresno or red jalapeño peppers, sliced into thin rings (about 4 cups [360 g])
- 2 teaspoons kosher salt

SPECIAL EQUIPMENT

- Blender

METHOD

Bring the vinegar, garlic, and honey to a boil in a small saucepan. Adjust the heat to a simmer and cook for 5 minutes. Remove from the heat and cool for 5 minutes.

Meanwhile, toss the peppers and salt together in a large bowl. Pour the cooled vinegar mixture over the peppers, stirring to coat. Cool to room temperature and then transfer to a container with a tight-fitting lid. Let stand at room temperature for 7 days to ferment. (If the garlic turns green or blue, the fermentation has gone bad. Discard and start again.)

Transfer the mixture to a blender and process into a sauce. (Don't worry if whole seeds remain.)

STORAGE

Refrigerate in a tightly sealed container for up to 1 month.

BISCUIT BAR

THIS BISCUIT BAR IS AN IDEA THAT ANDY *BORROWED* FROM HIS FRIEND AND FELLOW PIT MASTER AMY MILLS, WHO KNOWS HOW TO THROW A PARTY. HER BISCUIT BAR IS, FIRST AND FOREMOST, ALL ABOUT LIGHT, FLAKY BISCUITS THAT ARE SUBSTANTIAL ENOUGH TO TAKE A LOT OF JAM AND A LOT OF BUTTER. EVERY CHEF HAS HER OR HIS OWN RECIPE AND TECHNIQUE. ANDY AND WILL PERFECTED THEIRS THE ONLY WAY TWO SELF-RESPECTING BARBECUE GUYS WOULD: THROUGH A BISCUIT COMPETITION. WILL WON, ANDY ADMITS, WITH HIS EVERYTHING BISCUITS (PAGE 108). THEY HAVE ALL THE LAYERS OF A PERFECTLY FORMED CROISSANT AND THE SAVORY SPICE OF AN EVERYTHING BAGEL. IT'S A LABOR OF LOVE, WILL SAYS, WHO THINKS THE BEST BISCUITS ARE MADE BY HAND.

FROM THERE, IT'S UP TO YOUR GUESTS. EGGS IN A RING (PAGE 111) AND CITY HAM 2.0 (PAGE 53)? OR CHICKEN-FRIED STEAK (PAGE 114) AND SPICED HONEY BUTTER? OR ANY OTHER IMAGINATIVE COMBO THEY CAN COME UP WITH?

BISCUIT BAR MENU

Everything Biscuits (page 108)

Eggs in a Ring (page 111)

Boneless Fried Chicken (page 112)

Chicken-Fried Steak (page 114)

City Ham 2.0 (page 53)

Sliced American or cheddar cheese

Thinly sliced red onion

Romaine lettuce leaves

Spiced Honey Butter (page 116)

Strawberry-Cardamom Preserves (page 117)

Mayonnaise

Dijon mustard

Sriracha

EVERYTHING BISCUITS

INGREDIENTS

- 2½ cups (535 ml) heavy cream, divided
- ¼ cup (60 ml) apple cider vinegar
- 9 tablespoons (126 g) unsalted butter, frozen
- 5½ cups (688 g) all-purpose flour, plus more for dusting
- 4 teaspoons (18 g) baking powder
- 1 tablespoon (14 g) kosher salt
- ¾ cup (175 g) vegetable shortening, chilled and cut into pieces
- 1 batch Everything Mix (below)

SPECIAL EQUIPMENT

- Parchment paper
- Food processor
- Pastry brush

METHOD

Preheat the oven to 350°F (180°C, or gas mark 4). Line 2 sheet pans with parchment paper.

Whisk together 2¼ cups (535 ml) of the heavy cream and the vinegar in a bowl.

Grate the frozen butter using a food processor with a grater attachment or a cheese grater. Refrigerate until needed.

Whisk the flour, baking powder, and salt in a large bowl until evenly blended. Using your hands, toss the shortening with the flour to coat and then rub the pieces between your fingers to distribute evenly throughout the flour. Add the butter, tossing it to break up any clumps and distribute evenly so that the flour looks mealy. Work lightly and quickly to keep the mixture as cold as possible. Make a well in the center of the flour.

Whisk the cream and vinegar mixture again and pour it into the center of the flour. Use your hands to mix lightly and thoroughly until all the flour is evenly moistened; you may need another tablespoon or two (15 to 28 ml) more cream. Be careful not to overwork the dough. Gather the dough into a ball; it should be smooth and soft, not sticky or dry.

On a lightly floured surface, roll the dough out into a 1½-inch (3.8 cm)-thick, 5 × 12 ½-inch (13 × 31.5 cm) rectangle. With a floured cookie cutter or a knife, cut out as many 2½-inch (6.5 cm) square biscuits as possible. Gently reroll scraps for a total of 10 to 12 biscuits.

Divide the biscuits between the prepared sheet pans, spaced about 2 inches (5 cm) apart, and brush generously with the remaining heavy cream. (You may not need it all.) Top each biscuit with 1 teaspoon (4 g) of Everything Mix.

Bake until the biscuits are golden and cooked through, about 40 minutes, rotating the pans halfway through. Transfer to a wire rack to cool.

STORAGE

Store in a tightly sealed container for up to 24 hours.

EVERYTHING MIX

INGREDIENTS

- 1 tablespoon (8 g) sesame seeds
- 1 tablespoon (8 g) poppy seeds
- 2 teaspoons fennel seeds
- 1½ teaspoons cumin seeds
- 1 teaspoon dried onion flakes
- 1 teaspoon dried garlic flakes
- ¾ teaspoon flaky sea salt

METHOD

Combine everything in a bowl and mix thoroughly.

STORAGE

Store in a cool, dark place in an airtight container for up to 6 months.

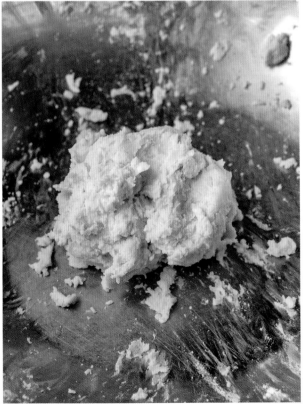

🕐 **ACTIVE TIME: 15 MINUTES | TOTAL TIME: 30 MINUTES | YIELD: 10 PIECES**

EGGS IN A RING

INGREDIENTS

- 10 large eggs
- 6 tablespoons (90 ml) whole milk
- 1½ teaspoons kosher salt
- ½ teaspoon finely ground black pepper

SPECIAL EQUIPMENT

- Ten 3-inch (7.5 cm) ring molds or Mason jar rings
- Nonstick spray

METHOD

In a small bowl, whisk the eggs with the milk, salt, and pepper until fully blended.

Preheat an electric griddle to 275°F (135°C) or heat a cast-iron pan over medium heat. Arrange the molds on the griddle at least 1 inch (2.5 cm) apart. Let the molds heat for 30 seconds. Spray the griddle and molds with nonstick spray, pour about 1 tablespoon (15 ml) of the egg mixture into each mold, and allow to cook briefly. This will keep the egg mixture from leaking out of the molds. Top each mold with another 3 tablespoons (45 ml) of egg mixture and cook for 3 minutes.

Drizzle about 2 tablespoons (28 ml) of water around the molds and cover with an inverted sheet pan for 5 minutes. Remove the pan and carefully flip the eggs. Cook for 2 minutes more.

Transfer the eggs to a work surface and remove the rings. If necessary, gently run a butter knife around the edge of the ring to loosen the eggs.

STORAGE

Refrigerate in a tightly sealed container for up to 2 days.

BONELESS FRIED CHICKEN

INGREDIENTS

- 10 boneless, skinless chicken thighs (about 3 ounces [85 g] each)
- 1 batch Buttermilk Brine (page 113)
- 3 cups (375 g) all-purpose flour
- 2¼ teaspoons (12 g) kosher salt, plus more for sprinkling
- ½ teaspoon baking powder
- 1½ teaspoons chili powder
- 1½ teaspoons garlic powder
- ¾ teaspoon dried thyme
- ½ teaspoon cayenne pepper
- ¼ teaspoon coarsely ground black pepper, plus more for sprinkling
- About 1 cup (235 ml) vegetable oil

SPECIAL EQUIPMENT

- Meat pounder
- Parchment paper
- Instant-read thermometer

METHOD

Trim the chicken thighs of fat. Place them between 2 pieces of plastic wrap and pound lightly to an even ¼-inch (6 mm) thickness. Place the chicken in the brine and refrigerate for 24 to 48 hours.

Combine the flour, salt, baking powder, and spices in a bowl, whisking to blend. Line a sheet pan with parchment paper.

One at a time, lift the chicken pieces from the brine, letting the excess run back into the bowl. Transfer to the flour dredge, turning and pressing gently to coat until there are no wet spots and then place on the sheet pan. Repeat with the remaining chicken, making sure the coated pieces are not touching each other. Refrigerate for 1 hour to set the coating. Reserve the remaining flour mixture.

When you are ready to fry the chicken, add oil to a skillet to a depth of ⅛ to ¼ inch (3 to 6 mm). Heat over medium-high heat. Place a paper towel–lined sheet pan beside the stove, along with the instant-read thermometer.

Remove the chicken from the refrigerator. When the oil is sizzling hot, dip 1 piece of chicken in the dredge again to coat, shake off the excess, and carefully lay it in the hot oil. Repeat with a few more pieces, leaving at least ½ inch (1.3 cm) of space between them, and fry until golden brown

on the bottom, 3 to 4 minutes. Turn and fry the second side until golden brown and cooked to an internal temperature of 165°F (74°C), about 3 minutes more. (If the chicken browns too quickly, adjust the heat to medium.) Transfer the cooked chicken to the paper towel–lined pan and repeat with the remaining chicken, working in batches to avoid crowding. Season lightly with salt and pepper.

STORAGE

Cool to room temperature, cover, and refrigerate for up to 1 day.

ACTIVE TIME: 10 MINUTES | **TOTAL TIME:** 1 HOUR 10 MINUTES PLUS 1 DAY | **YIELD:** 3 CUPS (700 ML)

BUTTERMILK BRINE

INGREDIENTS

- 1 cup (235 ml) water
- 4 cloves garlic, smashed
- 1 tablespoon (9 g) coarse pickling spice
- 2 teaspoons kosher salt
- 2 cups (475 ml) whole buttermilk
- ¼ cup (60 ml) Frank's RedHot
- 1 tablespoon (15 ml) white vinegar

SPECIAL EQUIPMENT

- Fine-mesh strainer

METHOD

Combine the water, garlic, pickling spice, and salt in a small saucepan over high heat and bring to a boil. Remove from the heat and cool to room temperature. Pour into a 1-quart (946 ml) container and add the buttermilk, Frank's RedHot, and vinegar. Cover and refrigerate for 24 hours. Strain out the spices before using.

STORAGE

Refrigerate the brine in a tightly sealed container for up to 1 week.

CHICKEN-FRIED STEAK

INGREDIENTS

- 1½ pounds (680 g) cube steak
- 1 batch Buttermilk Brine (page 113)
- 2 cups (250 g) all-purpose flour
- 1½ teaspoons kosher salt, plus more for sprinkling
- ¼ teaspoon baking powder
- 1 teaspoon chili powder
- 1 teaspoon garlic powder
- ½ teaspoon dried thyme
- ¼ teaspoon cayenne pepper
- ¼ teaspoon coarsely ground black pepper, plus more for sprinkling
- 3 large eggs
- About 1 cup (235 ml) vegetable oil

SPECIAL EQUIPMENT

- Parchment paper

METHOD

Cut the steak into ten 3-inch (7.5 cm) squares. Place the steak in the brine and refrigerate for 24 to 48 hours.

Combine the flour, salt, baking powder, and spices in a bowl, whisking to blend. In a separate bowl, whisk the eggs to blend. Line a sheet pan with parchment paper.

Remove the steaks from the brine and blot them as dry as possible with paper towels. Transfer a steak to the flour dredge, turning to coat. Shake off any excess flour and transfer to the eggs. Turn to coat and then lift out the steak, allowing the excess egg to drip back into the bowl. Return the steak to the flour dredge, turning and pressing gently to coat until there are no wet spots. Place the breaded steak on the sheet pan. Repeat with the remaining steaks, making sure the coated pieces are not touching. Along with the remaining flour dredge mixture, refrigerate for 2 hours to set the coating.

When you are ready to fry the steaks, add oil to a skillet to a depth of ⅛ inch (3 mm). Heat over medium-high heat. Place a paper towel–lined sheet pan beside the stove.

Remove the steaks from the refrigerator. When the oil is sizzling hot, dip a steak in the dredge again to coat, shake off the excess, and carefully lay it in the hot oil. Repeat with a few more pieces, leaving at least ½ inch (1.3 cm) of space between them, and fry until golden brown on the bottom, 2 to 3 minutes. Turn and fry the second side until golden brown, about 2 minutes more. (If the meat browns too quickly, adjust the heat to medium.) Transfer the cooked steaks to the paper towel–lined pan and repeat with the remaining pieces, working in batches to avoid crowding. Season lightly with salt and pepper.

STORAGE

Cool to room temperature, cover, and refrigerate in a tightly sealed container for up to 1 day.

WHAT THE BUTCHER KNOWS:

CUBE STEAK

WHAT IT IS: Typically, cube steak comes from a less expensive leg cut. It is then run through a cubing machine that uses blades to tenderize it.

WHAT TO ASK FOR: It's NAMP #1101, and you want thin slices, which are the most tender.

WHY TO CHOOSE IT: "Cube steak can really absorb seasoning," Ronnie says. Use it when you want the herbs and spices to be the star.

ACTIVE TIME: 5 MINUTES | TOTAL TIME: 5 MINUTES | YIELD: 1¼ CUPS (300 G)

SPICED HONEY BUTTER

INGREDIENTS

- 1 cup (225 g) unsalted butter, softened
- ¼ cup (85 g) honey
- ½ teaspoon kosher salt
- ½ teaspoon ground cinnamon
- ¼ teaspoon ground nutmeg
- ¼ teaspoon cayenne pepper
- 1 teaspoon flaky sea salt

SPECIAL EQUIPMENT

- Electric mixer

METHOD

Combine the butter, honey, salt, cinnamon, nutmeg, and cayenne pepper in a mixing bowl. Use an electric mixer to whip until smooth. Fold in the sea salt. Serve at room temperature.

STORAGE

Refrigerate in a tightly sealed container for up to 2 weeks. Bring to room temperature before serving.

ACTIVE TIME: 30 MINUTES | **TOTAL TIME:** 2 HOURS 30 MINUTES PLUS OVERNIGHT CHILL | **YIELD:** 2¼ CUPS (540 G)

STRAWBERRY-CARDAMOM PRESERVES

INGREDIENTS

- 4 cups (680 g) halved fresh strawberries
- 1 cup (200 g) sugar
- ¼ cup (85 g) honey
- 1 lemon, zested and juiced
- 1 tablespoon (15 ml) apple cider vinegar
- 2 teaspoons ground cardamom
- ¼ teaspoon dried thyme
- 1 teaspoon ground ginger
- ¼ teaspoon kosher salt

SPECIAL EQUIPMENT

- Deep-fry thermometer

METHOD

Combine the strawberries and sugar in a medium saucepan. Let stand for 2 hours.

Add the honey, lemon zest, vinegar, cardamom, thyme, ginger, and salt and stir to combine. Clip a thermometer to the side of the pan and place over medium heat and bring to a boil, stirring continually. Increase the heat to medium-high and boil, stirring constantly, until it reaches 220°F (104°C), about 5 minutes. Stir in the lemon juice and boil for 5 minutes more.

Cool the preserves to room temperature and transfer to a container with a tight-fitting lid. Refrigerate overnight.

STORAGE

Refrigerate in a tightly sealed container for up to 2 weeks.

BIG BRUNCH SALAD

ACTIVE TIME: 30 MINUTES
TOTAL TIME: 30 MINUTES
SERVES: 10 TO 12

A BRUNCH MENU WOULDN'T BE COMPLETE WITHOUT A SORTA HEALTHY OPTION, SOMETHING PEOPLE CAN PILE ON THEIR PLATES NEXT TO BISCUITS AND EGGS AND CHICKEN-FRIED STEAK TO MAKE THEM FEEL GOOD ABOUT THEIR CHOICES. THIS SALAD IS PERFECT FOR THAT: HEALTHY, BUT NOT *TOO* HEALTHY. YOU CAN CUSTOMIZE IT TO YOUR OWN TASTES (GREEN BEANS ARE A GREAT SUBSTITUTE FOR ASPARAGUS), BUT REMEMBER THAT THE KEY TO A TASTY AND BEAUTIFUL SALAD IS IN THE VARIETY OF SHAPES AND TEXTURES.

INGREDIENTS

- 2 bunches Lacinato kale, stemmed and thinly sliced crosswise (about 6 cups [402 g])
- 6 cups (180 g) baby spinach leaves
- ½ cup (120 g) canned chickpeas, drained and rinsed
- 2 tablespoons (10 g) shredded Parmesan cheese
- 1 batch Creamy Mustard Vinaigrette (page 110)
- 1 pint (283 g) cherry tomatoes, halved
- 2 medium carrots, peeled and shaved into ribbons with a vegetable peeler
- 1 small zucchini, sliced into half-moons
- 10 spears asparagus, cut into 1½-inch (3.8 cm) pieces
- 1 avocado, peeled, pitted, and diced
- ¼ cup (25 g) toasted sliced almonds

METHOD

Place the kale, spinach, chickpeas, and Parmesan cheese in a large mixing bowl. Add 1 to 2 tablespoons (15 to 28 ml) of vinaigrette, tossing just until the ingredients are evenly mixed and the leaves are shiny but not wet. Transfer the salad to a very large, shallow serving bowl or rimmed platter.

Scatter the remaining vegetables over the greens and top with the almonds. Drizzle about 2 tablespoons (28 ml) more dressing over the salad. Serve immediately, with the remaining dressing on the side.

STORAGE

Refrigerate prepared vegetables separately in tightly sealed containers for up to 2 days.

ACTIVE TIME: 10 MINUTES | **TOTAL TIME:** 10 MINUTES | **YIELD:** 1 ½ CUPS (355 ML)

CREAMY MUSTARD VINAIGRETTE

INGREDIENTS

- ¼ cup (60 g) Dijon mustard
- ¼ cup (60 ml) champagne vinegar or apple cider vinegar
- 2 tablespoons (28 g) Frank's RedHot
- 1 tablespoon (20 g) honey
- 2 teaspoons kosher salt
- ¾ cup (175 ml) extra virgin olive oil
- 2 tablespoons (30 g) sour cream

SPECIAL EQUIPMENT

- Food processor

METHOD

Combine the mustard, vinegar, hot sauce, honey, and salt in a food processor and blend until smooth. With the machine running, slowly drizzle in the oil. Process an additional 10 seconds to be sure the dressing has emulsified. Add the sour cream and pulse briefly to blend.

STORAGE

Refrigerate in a tightly sealed container for up to 5 days.

CRANBERRY LIME RICKEY

ACTIVE TIME: 10 MINUTES
TOTAL TIME: 1 HOUR 30 MINUTES
SERVES: 1

INGREDIENTS

- 1½ cups (355 ml) water
- 1 cup (100 g) fresh or (110 g) frozen cranberries
- 1 cup (200 g) sugar
- ¼ teaspoon kosher salt
- ¼ teaspoon dried rosemary leaves
- Ice cubes
- ¼ lime
- Club soda

SPECIAL EQUIPMENT

- Fine-mesh strainer

ANDY GREW UP SPENDING SUMMERS ON STAR ISLAND OFF THE COAST OF NEW HAMPSHIRE. ONE OF HIS FONDEST MEMORIES IS GETTING OFF THE ISLAND FERRY AND HEADING DIRECTLY TO THE SNACK BAR FOR A RASPBERRY LIME RICKEY. IT WAS SWEET, TART, LIGHT, AND REFRESHING. THIS CRANBERRY VERSION WAS INSPIRED—NO KIDDING—BY THANKSGIVING. GUESS ANDY WAS ALREADY TIRED OF THE NEW ENGLAND WINTER.

METHOD

To make the cranberry syrup, combine the water, cranberries, sugar, salt, and rosemary in a small saucepan over medium-high heat, stirring to dissolve the sugar. Bring to a boil and then adjust the heat to a simmer and cook for 15 minutes, stirring once or twice. Strain the syrup into a container with a lid, pressing on the fruit to break it but not to push it through the strainer; discard the solids. Cool to room temperature and then cover and refrigerate until cold. This will make more syrup than needed for 1 drink. Refrigerate extra syrup for up to 2 weeks.

Fill a 12-ounce (355 ml) glass with ice. Add 2 tablespoons (28 ml) of the cranberry syrup. Squeeze in the lime and drop it into the glass. Fill to the rim with club soda and serve with a straw.

BUBBLE THYME

ACTIVE TIME: 7 MINUTES
TOTAL TIME: 1 HOUR
SERVES: 1

INGREDIENTS

- ½ cup (100 g) sugar
- ½ cup (120 ml) water
- 2 tablespoons (40 g) honey
- 1 small bunch fresh thyme sprigs, divided
- 1 tablespoon (15 ml) fresh lemon juice
- ½ cup (120 ml) chilled Cava or Prosecco

SPECIAL EQUIPMENT

- Fine-mesh strainer

FOR BRUNCH, YOU WANT A LIGHT AND REFRESHING COCKTAIL, SOMETHING IT FEELS PERFECTLY APPROPRIATE TO DRINK BEFORE THE CLOCK STRIKES NOON. BUT YOU ALSO WANT SOMETHING MORE MEMORABLE THAN THE TYPICAL MIMOSA. THIS SIPPER HAS THE CITRUS AND BUBBLES OF THAT BRUNCH GO-TO, PLUS AN INTRIGUING TOUCH OF THYME.

METHOD

To make the thyme-honey syrup, combine the sugar, water, and honey in a small saucepan over medium heat, stirring until the sugar dissolves. Add most of the thyme, reserving a few sprigs for garnish. When the mixture comes to a boil, cook for 1 minute, and then remove from the heat. Set aside to steep for 30 minutes and then strain the liquid into a container with a tight-fitting lid. Chill until cold. This will make more syrup than needed for 1 drink. Refrigerate extra syrup for up to 2 weeks.

Combine 1½ tablespoons (25 ml) of the thyme-honey syrup and the lemon juice in a champagne flute. Add the sparkling wine, pouring slowly to prevent it from bubbling over. Stir gently and garnish with a fresh sprig of thyme.

SMOKIN' HOT MARY

ACTIVE TIME: 10 MINUTES
TOTAL TIME: 10 MINUTES
SERVES: 8 TO 10

INGREDIENTS

- 3½ cups (820 ml) tomato juice
- 1¼ cups (295 ml) bourbon or vodka
- 1 lemon, juiced (about ¼ cup [60 ml])
- 1 tablespoon (15 g) prepared horseradish
- 1 tablespoon (15 ml) Worcestershire sauce
- 1 tablespoon (7 g) Old Bay Seasoning
- 1½ teaspoons chipotle powder
- 1 teaspoon habanero hot sauce
- Ice cubes
- Spiced Pickle Chips (below), for garnish

THIS IS A BIG, BOLD BLOODY MARY WITH LOTS OF SPICE AND A SUBTLE SMOKINESS (FROM THE CHIPOTLE POWDER). SURE, YOU COULD USE THE TRADITIONAL VODKA WITH A CELERY STICK GARNISH HERE, BUT BOURBON AND PICKLES PLAY SO WELL WITH THESE BARBECUE FLAVORS. WE USE THE SPICED PICKLE CHIPS (BELOW) AS GARNISH AT THE SMOKE SHOP AND OUR GUESTS TRY TO ORDER THEM AS A SIDE. THEY ARE THAT GOOD.

METHOD

Combine the tomato juice, bourbon, lemon juice, horseradish, Worcestershire sauce, Old Bay, chipotle powder, and hot sauce in a 2-quart (1.9 L) pitcher; stir to blend. Serve over ice in 10-ounce (285 ml) glasses garnished with the pickle chips.

SPICED PICKLE CHIPS

ACTIVE TIME: 5 MINUTES
TOTAL TIME: 5 MINUTES
YIELD: ABOUT 30 PIECES

INGREDIENTS

- 1 jar (16 ounces, or 455 g) of bread-and-butter pickles
- 1 teaspoon chipotle powder
- 1 teaspoon Old Bay Seasoning

METHOD

Drain the pickles and spread them out on a paper towel–lined plate. Pat dry with more paper towels. Mix the spices together and sprinkle generously over the pickles. Set aside until ready to use.

STORAGE

Store in a sealed container for up to 3 days.

AMY'S PERFECT GLAZED PEACHES

ACTIVE TIME: 20 MINUTES

TOTAL TIME: 20 MINUTES

SERVES: 8

INGREDIENTS

- ½ cup (112 g) unsalted butter
- 1½ cups (340 g) packed dark brown sugar
- ¼ cup (60 ml) Bulleit bourbon or your favorite bourbon
- ½ teaspoon kosher salt, divided
- 4 ripe peaches, halved and pitted
- 2 cups (480 g) mascarpone cheese, at room temperature
- ½ cup (120 ml) heavy cream
- ½ teaspoon vanilla extract

AMY MILLS IS BARBECUE ROYALTY. SHE AND HER FATHER, MIKE, RUN THE FAMOUS 17TH STREET BARBECUE IN SOUTHERN ILLINOIS, AND AMY TRAVELS THE COUNTRY SHARING HER BBQ KNOWLEDGE. ANDY FIRST TASTED THIS DESSERT WHEN HE WAS JUDGING A TV COOKING COMPETITION. HE KNEW RIGHT AWAY WHO HAD MADE THE DISH. THERE'S NO SMOKER INVOLVED, BUT THE RECIPE CAPTURES AMY'S COOKING STYLE. IT'S CASUAL PERFECTION, WITH A SHOT OF BOURBON.

METHOD

Melt the butter in a large, heavy-bottomed sauté pan over medium heat. Add the brown sugar, bourbon, and ¼ teaspoon of the salt, stirring to melt the sugar. Cook, stirring occasionally, until bubbly and caramel colored, 5 to 10 minutes. Add the peach halves, reduce the heat to medium-low, and cook, turning occasionally to coat the peaches in syrup, until they are soft and glazed, 5 to 10 minutes.

Mix the mascarpone, heavy cream, vanilla, and remaining ¼ teaspoon salt in a small bowl. Using the back of a spoon, swipe the mixture on a serving tray. Place the glazed peaches on top of the mascarpone and drizzle a bit of the pan syrup over the top.

STORAGE

Refrigerate the peaches in their syrup and the mascarpone mixture separately for up to 4 days.

THE BERRY BUCKLE

ACTIVE TIME: 30 MINUTES

TOTAL TIME: 3 HOURS

SERVES: 12

INGREDIENTS

- 2¼ cups (281 g) all-purpose flour
- 2 teaspoons baking powder
- 1½ cups (337 g) unsalted butter, cut into pieces, at room temperature
- ⅓ cup (67 g) sugar
- 1 large egg
- 1½ teaspoons whole buttermilk
- 3½ cups (440 g) fresh raspberries
- 1½ cups (220 g) fresh blackberries
- 1 batch Pecan Streusel (page 127)

SPECIAL EQUIPMENT

- Stand mixer

CHEFS CAN'T HELP IT. THEY ALWAYS WANT TO TWEAK EVEN THE BEST RECIPES. NOT THIS ONE. SARAH'S BERRY BUCKLE CAN'T BE IMPROVED. IN FACT, ITS ONLY DOWNFALL (IF YOU CAN CALL IT THAT) IS THAT IT REQUIRES FARMERS MARKET–FRESH BERRIES. (FROZEN BERRIES ARE TOO WATERY; OFF-SEASON BERRIES ARE JUST SAD.) THIS SHOULD BE THE DISH YOU THINK OF WHEN YOU SPOT THE FIRST OF THE RASPBERRIES AND BLACKBERRIES EACH SUMMER.

METHOD

Preheat the oven to 350°F (180°C, or gas mark 4). Place an 8-inch (20 cm) square baking pan on a sheet pan in case of any overflow.

Whisk the flour and baking powder together in a medium bowl and set aside.

Combine the butter and sugar in the bowl of a stand mixer fitted with a paddle attachment and beat on medium speed until light and fluffy, 3 to 5 minutes. Add the egg and beat until well combined, scraping down the bowl as needed. On low speed, add the flour mixture in 2 additions, alternating with the buttermilk. Scrape down the bowl occasionally to be sure no dry flour remains. Transfer the batter to the baking pan; be sure to scrape the bowl and paddle clean. Spread the batter in an even layer in the bottom of the baking dish. Scatter the berries evenly on top. Pour the streusel topping over the berries, spreading until the fruit is evenly covered. The pan will be very full.

Bake the buckle until it is golden brown on the top and bottom and tests clean in the center, about 1 hour.

Cool for at least 1½ hours before cutting into 12 pieces. Serve from the pan.

STORAGE

Cover and store at room temperature for up to 2 days. Refrigerate for up to 4 days.

PECAN STREUSEL

ACTIVE TIME: 5 MINUTES
TOTAL TIME: 5 MINUTES
YIELD: 3 CUPS (542 G)

INGREDIENTS

- 1 cup (125 g) all-purpose flour
- ¾ cup (170 g) packed light brown sugar
- ½ cup (100 g) granulated sugar
- ½ cup (50 g) pecans, toasted and chopped
- ¾ teaspoon ground nutmeg
- ¼ teaspoon ground cinnamon
- ½ cup (112 g) unsalted butter, cut into pieces, at room temperature

SPECIAL EQUIPMENT

- Stand mixer

METHOD

Place the flour, sugars, pecans, nutmeg, and cinnamon in the bowl of a stand mixer bowl fitted with a paddle attachment and beat to combine. Add the butter and mix on the lowest speed just until evenly distributed and the mixture looks like wet sand, about 1 minute. Do not overbeat; the mixture should be granular, not creamy.

STORAGE

Store in tightly sealed container and refrigerate for 1 week or freeze for up to 3 months.

THE FANCY
PARTY

YOU MIGHT HAVE NOTICED THAT WE LIKE TO KEEP THINGS CASUAL AROUND HERE. OUR PARTIES ARE USUALLY COME-AS-YOU-ARE AFFAIRS WITH DELIGHTFULLY MESSY FOOD MEANT FOR EATING WITH YOUR HANDS. BUT SOME-TIMES—GRADUATIONS, WEDDINGS, BABY SHOWERS, THE KENTUCKY DERBY—WE LIKE TO PUT ON OUR SEERSUCKER AND PUT DOWN THE SOLO CUPS.

For these gatherings, we break out our best-dressed recipes, too. Good cooking is good cooking, of course, no matter how big the hats on your guests, but how you present the food can really change the vibe of a party. These special occasions call for dramatic dishes like Beef Prime Rib au Jus (page 135) or a whole side of smoked salmon (page 138). They call for a cocktail that sparkles with (real!) silver and gold (see page 151).

This is the time to iron the tablecloths, dust off the china, and create the Instagram-perfect centerpiece. (Don't worry, our friend and party designer extraordinaire Taniya Nayak will walk you through it, page 153.)

But don't ever get so caught up in the fancy that you forget the point of a party: fun.

HAM AND RICE CROQUETTES

INGREDIENTS

- 6 large eggs, divided
- 4 cups (744 g) cooked white rice, at room temperature
- 1½ cups (225 g) diced City Ham 2.0 (page 53)
- 3 cups (150 g) panko breadcrumbs, divided
- 1 cup (100 g) grated Parmesan cheese
- 1 cup (115 g) grated dill Havarti cheese
- ¼ cup (5 g) dried parsley
- 2 teaspoons kosher salt, plus more to taste
- 1½ teaspoons coarsely ground black pepper
- 6 cups (1.4L) vegetable oil
- Fermented Honey Hot Sauce (page 105) or your favorite mustard, for serving

SPECIAL EQUIPMENT

- Deep-fry thermometer

ANDY'S BEEN MAKING THESE CROQUETTES SINCE HIS CULINARY SCHOOL DAYS. HE LEARNED EARLY ON THAT YOU JUST CAN'T GO WRONG WITH HAM AND CHEESE, FRIED. THESE ARE A GREAT CHOICE FOR A PARTY BECAUSE THEY CAN BE MADE A FEW DAYS IN ADVANCE AND FRIED QUICKLY JUST BEFORE THE PARTY. PLUS, THEY LOOK MUCH HARDER TO PREPARE THAN THEY REALLY ARE. (WE PROMISE NOT TO TELL YOUR GUESTS.)

METHOD

In a large bowl, beat 3 of the eggs until well blended. Add the rice, ham, 1 cup (50 g) of the panko, cheeses, parsley, salt, and pepper and mix until thoroughly combined. The mixture should hold together when squeezed.

Attach a deep-fry thermometer to the side of a large heavy-bottomed pan and add oil to a depth of 1½ inches (3.8 cm). Place the pan over medium-high heat. Place a paper towel–lined sheet pan beside the stove.

While the oil is heating, form the croquettes. Scoop about ¼ cup (60 ml) of the mixture into your hand and shape it into a 1½-inch-long by ¾-inch-wide (3.8 by 2 cm) cylinder with flat ends. Repeat with the remaining rice mixture to make 30 croquettes.

Beat the remaining 3 eggs in a shallow bowl until well blended. Put the remaining 2 cups (100 g) of panko in another shallow bowl. One at a time, dip the croquettes into the egg, allowing the excess to drip back into the bowl, and then transfer to the panko, turning and pressing gently to coat.

When the oil reaches 350°F (180°C), carefully transfer the croquettes to the pan, working in batches to avoid crowding. Fry, turning occasionally, until golden brown, 3 to 5 minutes. Transfer the finished croquettes to the paper towel–lined pan to drain; season lightly with salt. Cool for a few minutes before serving with Fermented Honey Hot Sauce or your favorite mustard for dipping.

STORAGE

The breaded croquettes can be refrigerated uncooked for up to 3 days. They should be fried immediately before serving.

DEVILED EGGS WITH SMOKED FISH

ACTIVE TIME: 30 MINUTES

TOTAL TIME: 1 HOUR

SERVES: 10 TO 12 (24 PIECES)

INGREDIENTS

- 5 quarts (4.7 L) cold water, divided
- Ice cubes
- 12 large eggs
- ½ cup (112 g) kosher salt
- ¼ cup (60 g) mayonnaise
- 2 tablespoons (22 g) yellow mustard
- 1 teaspoon cayenne pepper
- 1 teaspoon garlic powder
- ½ teaspoon chipotle powder
- 4 ounces (115 g) smoked salmon or trout

SPECIAL EQUIPMENT

- Food processor
- Pastry bag with star tip

WILL WAS VERY LEERY OF MESSING WITH THE CLASSIC DEVILED EGG. THERE'S A REASON THESE DELICIOUS BITES ARE SERVED AT EVERY PROPER PARTY. HE SETTLED ON JUST DRESSING THEM UP WITH A LITTLE SMOKED SALMON OR TROUT, WHICH ACCENTUATES THE FLAVOR OF THE EGG. AND HE RELIES ON AN AGE-OLD KITCHEN TRICK: BUY YOUR EGGS A WEEK BEFORE YOU PLAN TO BOIL THEM. IT MAKES THEM EASIER TO PEEL.

METHOD

Stir together about 2 quarts (1.9 L) of the water and 2 cups of ice in a large bowl for an ice bath.

Cover the eggs with the remaining 3 quarts (2.8 L) of cold water in a pot large enough to hold the eggs in a single layer and add the salt. Cover the pot and bring just to a boil over medium-high heat; remove from the heat and allow to stand, covered, for 13 minutes. Transfer the eggs to the ice bath and allow to cool for 5 minutes.

Peel the eggs by gently cracking each shell against a flat surface and returning the eggs to the ice bath; water will seep underneath the shells and make them easier to remove. Gently slip off the shells, swish in the ice bath to remove any particles, and dry the peeled eggs on paper towels.

Cut each egg in half lengthwise and gently remove the yolks. Put the yolks in the food processor bowl and arrange the whites on a serving platter. Pulse the yolks to produce fluffy, evenly sized crumbs. Add the mayonnaise, mustard, cayenne pepper, garlic powder, and chipotle powder and

pulse until evenly blended and smooth. Transfer the egg yolk mixture to a pastry bag fitted with a star tip. Pipe the filling into the egg whites and garnish with smoked fish.

STORAGE

The hard-boiled eggs can be peeled and refrigerated in a tightly sealed container for up to 2 days. Refrigerate assembled deviled eggs in a tightly sealed container for up to 1 day.

SMOKED SHRIMP COCKTAIL

ACTIVE TIME: 25 MINUTES
TOTAL TIME: 7 HOURS
SERVES: 10 TO 12 (33 PIECES)

MOST PEOPLE SERVE SHRIMP COCKTAIL WITH COCKTAIL SAUCE, BUT ANDY GREW UP WORKING AT A *FANCY* RESTAURANT THAT PAIRED SHRIMP AND REMOULADE. IT'S A LITTLE MORE MELLOW, WITH SALTY POPS OF PICKLE. IT LETS THE SHRIMP REALLY SHINE.

INGREDIENTS

- 4 cups (946 ml) water
- 2 tablespoons (28 g) kosher salt
- 1 tablespoon (6 g) Creole Spice (page 69) or your favorite "boil" spices
- 4 cloves garlic, smashed
- 3 pounds (1.4 kg) extra-large (U-12) raw shrimp, peeled and deveined
- Remoulade (below), for serving

SPECIAL EQUIPMENT

- Smoker and accessories (see page 212)
- Oak or your favorite hardwood

METHOD

To make the brine, bring the water to a boil in a small saucepan over high heat. Add the salt, Creole Spice, and garlic and stir until dissolved. Remove from the heat and cool to room temperature and then refrigerate until cold, at least 2 hours.

Place the shrimp in a bowl and pour the brine over them, making sure they are fully submerged. Cover and refrigerate for 2 to 4 hours, but no longer.

While the shrimp are brining, preheat your smoker to 225°F (107°C). About 30 minutes before you are ready to cook, stoke the fire with your favorite hardwood; we prefer oak for this. (See page 212 for additional information on preparing a smoker.)

Drain the shrimp. Toss the shrimp with any spices that remain in the bowl after draining and smoke until they are opaque throughout, 14 to 16 minutes. (If possible, remove the smoker rack to arrange the shrimp.) Remove from the smoker and transfer to a wire rack for 5 minutes and then refrigerate until cold, at least 3 hours. Transfer to a tightly sealed container and refrigerate until ready to serve with the Remoulade.

STORAGE

Refrigerate in a tightly sealed container for up to 2 days.

REMOULADE

ACTIVE TIME: 15 MINUTES
TOTAL TIME: 15 MINUTES
YIELD: 1½ CUPS (350 G)

INGREDIENTS

- ½ cup (115 g) mayonnaise
- 6 tablespoons (90 g) Dijon mustard
- ¼ cup (60 g) whole-grain mustard
- 2 tablespoons (20 g) minced red onion
- ½ dill pickle spear, minced (about 2 tablespoons [18 g])
- 1 tablespoon (15 ml) dill pickle juice
- 1 tablespoon (15 g) ketchup
- 1½ teaspoons prepared horseradish
- 1½ teaspoons capers
- 1 clove garlic, minced
- ¼ teaspoon cayenne pepper
- ¼ teaspoon kosher salt

METHOD

Combine all the ingredients in a bowl. Cover and refrigerate until needed.

STORAGE

Refrigerate in a tightly sealed container for 5 to 7 days.

BEEF PRIME RIB AU JUS

ACTIVE TIME: 30 MINUTES
TOTAL TIME: 5 HOURS 30 MINUTES
SERVES: 10 TO 12

INGREDIENTS

- 8- to 10-pound (3.6 to 4.6 kg) beef prime rib roast, frenched (trimmings reserved)
- 1 cup (224 g) kosher salt
- 1 cup (96 g) coarsely ground black pepper
- 16 cloves garlic, divided
- 3 tablespoons (5 g) roughly chopped fresh rosemary
- 2 tablespoons (28 ml) Worcestershire sauce
- 2 tablespoons (22 g) yellow mustard
- 2 large shallots, roughly chopped
- 1 large carrot, sliced ½ inch (1.3 cm) thick
- 2 stalks celery, cut into ½-inch (1.3 cm) pieces
- 3 tablespoons (48 g) tomato paste
- 3 tablespoons (45 ml) extra virgin olive oil
- 2 sprigs fresh thyme
- 2 sprigs fresh sage
- 1 cup (235 ml) red wine
- 6 cups (1.4 L) low-sodium beef broth

SPECIAL EQUIPMENT

- Smoker and accessories (see page 212)
- Post oak or your favorite hardwood
- Food processor
- Probe thermometer
- Fine-mesh strainer

WHEN YOU COOK MEAT LOW AND SLOW, IT DEVELOPS DEEP FLAVOR AND A TENDER, JUICY TEXTURE. BUT WHEN YOU COOK IT HOT AND FAST, YOU GET A BEAUTIFUL, DARK CRUST WITH A SATISFYING BITE. THIS IMPRESSIVE DISH USES BOTH METHODS, A GENTLE SMOKE FOLLOWED BY A BRIEF STAY IN AN OVEN CRANKED AS HIGH AS IT CAN GO.

METHOD

Remove the roast from the refrigerator 1 hour before you intend to smoke it. This will ensure a faster cook time. Preheat your smoker to 275°F (135°C). About 30 minutes before you are ready to cook, stoke the fire with your favorite hardwood; we prefer post oak for this. (See page 212 for additional information on preparing a smoker.)

Combine the salt, pepper, 12 cloves of the garlic, rosemary, Worcestershire sauce, and mustard in a food processor. Blend for 30 seconds, scrape down the sides of the work bowl, and blend for 30 seconds more. Transfer the wet rub to a bowl.

This is messy, so we recommend seasoning the roast outside: Place the roast on a sheet pan and use your hands to spread the wet rub liberally and evenly on all sides of the meat, starting with the underside.

Smash the remaining 4 cloves of garlic and place in a baking pan along with the beef trimmings, shallots, carrot, celery, tomato paste, olive oil, and herbs. Stir to coat with the oil. Place the roast in the center of the smoker and put the baking pan underneath the roast to catch the drippings. Insert the thermometer probe horizontally into the thinner side of the muscle without touching the bone. Set the alarm temperature to 110°F

(43°C) for medium-rare or 115°F (46°C) for medium. Close the smoker and keep the temperature at a steady 275° (135°C) for approximately 2 hours 45 minutes.

When the roast is nearly done, preheat your oven to 500°F (250°C, or gas mark 10). When the roast is ready, remove it from the smoker and place it on a roasting rack set over a sheet pan. Allow it to rest for 5 minutes while you remove the baking pan with the drippings from the smoker. Place the baking pan over medium-high heat and add the wine. Bring to a boil, scraping any caramelized pieces from the bottom of the pan. Transfer the contents to a medium saucepan and boil for 2 minutes. Add the beef broth and adjust the heat to simmer for 40 minutes. Strain the jus and keep it warm.

Meanwhile, roast the meat for 20 minutes; the internal temperature will rise to about 125°F (52°C). Remove and rest the meat for 5 minutes. To serve, slice the prime rib into steaks. Place the prime rib bone-side down on a cutting board. Using a chef's knife, cut off the fat cap at the top of the bones. Next, slice along each bone following the curves of the bone using short cuts until the meat is removed. This will produce 12 boneless steaks. Serve with a gravy boat filled with jus.

CONTINUED

STORAGE

Refrigerate the wet rub in a tightly sealed container for up to 5 days. Refrigerate the jus in a tightly sealed container for up to 5 days. Wrap any leftover meat tightly in plastic wrap and refrigerate for up to 5 days or freeze for up to 3 months.

WHAT THE BUTCHER KNOWS:

PRIME RIB

WHAT IT IS: It's not necessarily prime. These days, when people use the word *prime*, they are typically referring to "USDA Prime," the rating given to the best marbled meats. The "prime" in "prime rib" refers to the fact that the flavorful rib section of the cow has long been the most desirable.

WHAT TO ASK FOR: You want NAMP #107 or 109, frenched. "Frenched" means that the butcher will cut away the meat and fat between the bones. But don't throw away all that flavor! The trimmings can be used in other recipes.

WHY TO CHOOSE IT: "It's impressive," Ronnie says. And it's both flavorful and tender.

SALMON SIDE WITH CUCUMBER CHOW-CHOW

ACTIVE TIME: 30 MINUTES

TOTAL TIME: 14 HOURS 30 MINUTES
TO 16 HOURS 30 MINUTES

SERVES: 8 TO 10

ANDY GREW UP IN SEATTLE EATING SALMON. HE CALLS IT "THE KING OF FISH," AND YOU'LL UNDERSTAND WHY WHEN YOU TASTE THIS VERSION. BRINING THE SALMON KEEPS IT MOIST THROUGH THE SMOKE, AND ALDER WOOD ADDS A SUBTLE, SWEET FLAVOR. THE CUCUMBER CHOW-CHOW ADDS A CRISP AND VINEGARY COUNTERPOINT. BE SURE TO START THE CHOW-CHOW AT LEAST 8 HOURS IN ADVANCE; IT'S EVEN BETTER AFTER A DAY OR TWO.

INGREDIENTS

- 8 cups (1.9 L) water
- 1 cup (225 g) packed light brown sugar
- ½ cup (112 g) kosher salt
- ¼ cup (60 ml) fish sauce
- 2 cloves garlic, smashed
- 2 teaspoons whole black peppercorns
- 1 side salmon (about 3 pounds [1.4 kg]), skin on, pin bones removed
- 1 batch Salmon Rub (page 140)
- 2 lemons, cut into ⅛-inch (3 mm)-thick slices
- 1 bunch curly parsley
- 1 batch Cucumber Chow-Chow (page 140)

SPECIAL EQUIPMENT

- Smoker and accessories (see page 212)
- Alder or your favorite hardwood
- Nonstick spray
- Probe thermometer

METHOD

To make the brine, bring the water to a boil in a medium saucepan over high heat. Add the sugar, salt, fish sauce, garlic, and peppercorns and stir until the sugar and salt have dissolved. Remove from the heat and cool to room temperature and then refrigerate until cold, at least 12 hours.

Place the salmon in a shallow container long enough to hold it flat and deep enough to submerge the salmon. Pour the chilled brine over the salmon and refrigerate for 2 to 4 hours.

While the salmon is brining, preheat your smoker to 225°F (107°C). About 30 minutes before you are ready to cook, stoke the fire with your favorite hardwood; we prefer alder or apple wood for this. (See page 212 for additional information on preparing a smoker.)

Coat a sheet pan large enough to hold the salmon with nonstick spray. Remove the salmon from the brine, pat it dry with paper towels, and place it skin-side down on the sheet pan. Sprinkle the flesh evenly with the Salmon Rub.

Insert the thermometer probe into the thickest part of the salmon. Place the sheet pan in the smoker and smoke to an internal temperature of 135°F (57°C), about 30 minutes. Remove and allow the fish to rest on the pan for 5 minutes before serving.

Garnish with lemon slices and parsley sprigs. Spoon a line of Cucumber Chow-Chow along the center of the salmon lengthwise and serve the rest on the side.

STORAGE

Refrigerate in a tightly sealed container for up to 2 days.

SALMON RUB

ACTIVE TIME: 5 MINUTES
TOTAL TIME: 5 MINUTES
YIELD: ABOUT ¼ CUP (30 G)

INGREDIENTS

- 1 tablespoon (15 g) light brown sugar
- 2 teaspoons kosher salt
- 2 teaspoons Old Bay Seasoning
- 2 teaspoons coarsely ground black pepper
- 1 teaspoon dried thyme

METHOD

Combine all the ingredients in a small bowl.

STORAGE

Store in a cool, dark place in an airtight container for up to several months.

CUCUMBER CHOW-CHOW

ACTIVE TIME: 30 MINUTES
TOTAL TIME: 8 HOURS 30 MINUTES
YIELD: ABOUT 10 CUPS (1.5 KG)

INGREDIENTS

- ½ cup (120 ml) dill pickle juice
- 2 tablespoons (28 ml) olive oil
- 2 cloves garlic, minced
- 2 teaspoons ground cumin
- 2 teaspoons red pepper flakes
- 2 teaspoons coarsely ground black pepper, plus more for sprinkling
- 1 teaspoon kosher salt, plus more for sprinkling
- ¼ head savoy cabbage, diced (about 3 cups [210 g])
- 1 English cucumber, diced (about 2½ cups [338 g])
- 1 medium red onion, diced (about 2 cups [320 g])
- 1 red bell pepper, diced (about 1½ cups [225 g])
- 2 dill pickles, diced (about 1 cup [143 g])
- ½ cup (8 g) roughly chopped cilantro

METHOD

Combine the dill pickle juice, olive oil, garlic, cumin, red pepper flakes, black pepper, and salt in a large bowl and give it a good stir. Add the cabbage, cucumber, onion, red bell pepper, pickles, and cilantro and mix well. Cover and refrigerate for 8 hours, stirring every couple of hours. Season to taste with salt and pepper.

STORAGE

Refrigerate in a tightly sealed container for up to 3 days.

ROASTED ASPARAGUS WITH PEACH-SHALLOT VINAIGRETTE

ACTIVE TIME: 30 MINUTES

TOTAL TIME: 1 HOUR

SERVES: 10 TO 12 (GENEROUS
2 CUPS [425 G] VINAIGRETTE)

THIS ROASTED ASPARAGUS DESERVES A BEST-DRESSED AWARD. THE CHUNKY SWEET-SOUR-SAVORY VINAIGRETTE GIVES THE SLENDER SPEARS A POP OF SUMMER COLOR—AND IT IS GOOD ENOUGH TO EAT WITH A SPOON.

INGREDIENTS

- 3 small peaches, peeled and diced (about 2 cups [308 g])
- 2 shallots, diced small (about ½ cup [80 g])
- 1 tablespoon (15 ml) champagne vinegar
- 3 tablespoons (45 ml) extra virgin olive oil, divided
- 2 tablespoons (4 g) roughly chopped tarragon leaves
- ½ teaspoon kosher salt, plus more for sprinkling
- ½ teaspoon coarsely ground black pepper, plus more for sprinkling
- ½ teaspoon dried thyme
- 4 bunches asparagus, bottoms trimmed

METHOD

Preheat the oven to 475°F (240°C, or gas mark 9).

While the oven is heating, combine the peaches, shallots, vinegar, 1 tablespoon (15 ml) of the olive oil, tarragon, salt, pepper, and the thyme in a medium bowl and mix well. Refrigerate until needed.

Divide the asparagus between 2 large sheet pans, spreading in a single layer. (Cook the asparagus in batches if necessary, to avoid crowding.) Drizzle each pan with about 1 tablespoon (15 ml) of olive oil and sprinkle with some salt and pepper. Roast until the asparagus are lightly browned and give up a bit of juice if you squeeze the cut end, 8 to 10 minutes. If you aren't sure about doneness, taste a spear; it should be just past al dente.

Transfer the asparagus neatly to a serving platter. Spoon the vinaigrette in a line across the center, perpendicular to the spears. Serve at room temperature.

STORAGE

Refrigerate the vinaigrette in a tightly sealed container for up to 2 days. The asparagus can be cooked and quickly chilled up to 1 day in advance.

BRISKET FAT WHIPPED POTATOES

ACTIVE TIME: 1 HOUR 30 MINUTES

TOTAL TIME: 4 HOURS 30 MINUTES

SERVES: 10 TO 12

INGREDIENTS

- 1 pound (455 g) brisket fat or other solid beef fat
- 2 tablespoons (28 ml) water
- 2 small sweet onions, thinly sliced (about 4 cups [640 g])
- 5 tablespoons (70 g) kosher salt, divided
- 1 cup (235 ml) heavy cream
- ½ cup (112 g) unsalted butter
- 3 pounds (1.4 kg) russet potatoes (all about the same size), peeled
- 2½ quarts (2.4 L) cold water

SPECIAL EQUIPMENT

- Smoker and accessories (see page 212)
- Oak or your favorite hardwood
- Blender

THE FAMOUS FRENCH CHEF JOËL ROBUCHON MADE HIS MARK WITH, OF ALL THINGS, THE WORLD'S MOST DECADENT MASHED POTATOES: 2 PARTS POTATO TO 1 PART BUTTER. THIS IS THE PIT MASTER'S VERSION OF POMMES ROBUCHON, MADE WITH LEFTOVER BRISKET FAT (OR WHATEVER FAT YOU HAVE ON HAND).

METHOD

Preheat the smoker to 250°F (121°C). About 30 minutes before you are ready to cook, stoke the fire with your favorite hardwood; we prefer oak for this. (See page 212 for additional information on preparing a smoker.)

Place the brisket fat on the top rack of your smoker. Place a baking pan below to catch the rendered fat. Smoke for 1 hour.

Place the solid fat in the drip pan and remove it from the smoker. When the fat is cool enough to handle, cut it into chunks and transfer to a medium saucepan along with the rendered fat from the drip pan. Add the water and bring to a gentle boil over medium-high heat. Cover the pan and adjust the heat to simmer for 30 minutes. Stir every 5 minutes to ensure the fat is not burning.

Discard any solid fat left in the pan and bring the rendered fat to a boil. (There will be about 1½ cups [355 ml].) Add the onions and 3 tablespoons (42 g) of the salt, reduce the heat to low, and cook for 15 minutes, stirring continually to prevent burning. The onions will cook down and become translucent; do not let them brown. Add the cream and butter and cook over medium heat until slightly thickened, about

5 minutes. Remove from the heat and allow to cool slightly, about 10 minutes. Transfer the liquid to a blender and process for 1 minute; some onion bits may remain. Return the mixture to the saucepan and keep warm while you cook the potatoes.

Place the potatoes, cold water, and remaining 2 tablespoons (28 g) of salt in a large saucepan. Bring to a boil and then adjust the heat so the water simmers. Cook until the potatoes are fork tender, about 30 minutes. Drain the potatoes well and allow to air-dry for 5 minutes. Rice or mash the potatoes in the saucepan. Fold in the warm fat mixture, stirring until fully incorporated. Place the pan over low heat and stir to warm the potatoes. Serve immediately.

STORAGE

Refrigerate in a tightly sealed container for up to 4 days. Reheat over low heat, stirring every few minutes. Additional milk or cream may be needed.

FANCY CORNBREAD

ACTIVE TIME: 20 MINUTES

TOTAL TIME: 1 HOUR

SERVES: 12 TO 16

THIS IS NOT FOR THE PURIST. IF YOU ARE A CORNBREAD TRADITIONALIST, STOP READING NOW. FOR THOSE WHO LIKE TO TAKE THE UNEATEN PATH, THOUGH, THIS IS A SPECTACULAR RECIPE, WITH THE CRUNCH OF FRESH CORN AND WARM, RUSTIC SOUTHWESTERN FLAVORS. ANDY'S BEEN MAKING IT FOR THIRTY YEARS.

INGREDIENTS

- 3½ cups (438 g) all-purpose flour
- 2 cups (275 g) coarse yellow cornmeal
- 2 tablespoons (28 g) baking powder
- 1½ teaspoons ground cumin
- 1½ teaspoons kosher salt
- 1 teaspoon ground cinnamon
- ½ teaspoon cayenne pepper
- 3 scallions (green part only), chopped (about ¼ cup [25 g])
- ½ cup (112 g) unsalted butter, softened
- 1 cup (200 g) sugar
- 2 large eggs
- 2 cups (475 ml) whole buttermilk
- 2 cups (308 g) fresh corn kernels (from 3 to 4 large ears)
- Spiced Honey Butter (page 116), for serving

SPECIAL EQUIPMENT

- Stand mixer

METHOD

Preheat the oven to 400°F (200°C, or gas mark 6). Grease a 13 × 9-inch (33 × 23 cm) baking pan.

Whisk together the flour, cornmeal, baking powder, cumin, salt, cinnamon, and cayenne pepper in a large bowl. Mix in the scallions and set aside.

In the bowl of a stand mixer fitted with a paddle attachment, cream the butter and sugar on medium speed until light and fluffy, about 2 minutes. Add the eggs, one at a time, blending well after each. With the mixer on low speed, add the buttermilk slowly to avoid splashing. Add the dry ingredients in 3 batches, mixing on low speed after each addition and scraping down the sides of the bowl with a rubber spatula each time. Add the corn on low speed, mixing just to incorporate.

Spread the batter in the prepared pan and bake until it begins to brown and a skewer inserted near the center comes out clean, 30 to 40 minutes. Let cool in the pan for 10 minutes and then turn out onto a wire rack. Cut into squares and serve hot with Spiced Honey Butter.

STORAGE

Store in a tightly sealed container for up to 3 days.

SUMMER TOMATO SALAD

ACTIVE TIME: 1 HOUR

TOTAL TIME: 2 HOURS 30 MINUTES

SERVES: 10 TO 12

INGREDIENTS

- 12 large, ripe plum tomatoes, sliced into ¼-inch (6 mm) rounds
- 4 large shallots, thinly sliced
- 4 cloves garlic, thinly sliced
- 3 tablespoons (45 ml) extra virgin olive oil
- 1 tablespoon (14 g) kosher salt
- 1 tablespoon (15 ml) red wine vinegar
- 2 teaspoons coarsely ground black pepper
- ¾ cup (116 g) fresh corn kernels
- 2 medium zucchini, sliced into very thin rounds
- 2 medium summer squash, sliced into very thin rounds
- ½ cup (40 g) shaved Parmesan cheese
- ¼ cup (6 g) torn basil
- ¼ cup (9 g) torn mint leaves
- 1 batch Olive Crisps (page 150)

SPECIAL EQUIPMENT

- Smoker and accessories (see page 212)
- Cherry or apple wood or your favorite hardwood
- Perforated pan

WHEN PRESENTED WITH RIPE TOMATOES, JUST-PICKED ZUCCHINI, AND LOCAL CORN, THE CHEF'S JOB IS TO KEEP THINGS SIMPLE AND LET THE SUMMER PRODUCE SHINE. BUT THAT DOESN'T MEAN YOU CAN'T GO ALL OUT ON THE PRESENTATION. THIS DISH WILL WOW YOUR GUESTS WITH ITS ELEGANT DESIGN. (FUN FACT: WILL GOT THE INSPIRATION FOR THIS FROM HIS FAVORITE MOVIE, *RATATOUILLE*, WHICH STARS AN ADORABLE RAT NAMED REMY WHO IMPRESSES A RESTAURANT CRITIC WITH A DISH A LOT LIKE THIS ONE.)

METHOD

Preheat your smoker to 275°F (135°C). About 30 minutes before you are ready to cook, stoke the fire with your favorite hardwood; we prefer cherry or apple wood for this. (See page 212 for additional information on preparing a smoker.)

Gently toss the tomatoes, shallots, garlic, olive oil, and salt in a large bowl. Allow to stand for 30 minutes. Arrange the tomatoes in a perforated pan and pour any juices from the bowl into a baking pan; reserve the shallots and garlic. Place the tomatoes in the smoker with the baking pan below to catch the drippings. Smoke the tomatoes for 15 minutes and then remove the drip pan, set the perforated pan with the tomatoes on top, and cool for 10 minutes. Add the vinegar, pepper, and corn to the juices in the baking pan and mix well to make a dressing.

On a large round platter, shingle the smoked tomatoes, zucchini, and summer squash in a neat, overlapping circle around the perimeter of the platter. Repeat with a second row inside the first and so on, to fill up the platter. You'll probably have enough vegetables to create two platters like this. Scatter with the reserved shallots and garlic. Spoon the dressing lightly over the vegetables. Top with the Parmesan cheese and herbs. Just before serving, scatter shards of Olive Crisps over the salad.

STORAGE

Refrigerate in a tightly sealed container for up to 3 days.

OLIVE CRISPS

ACTIVE TIME: 30 MINUTES
TOTAL TIME: 1 HOUR 15 MINUTES
YIELD: 10 TO 12 PIECES

INGREDIENTS

- 15 pitted Kalamata olives, halved lengthwise and thinly sliced
- ½ cup (63 g) all-purpose flour
- ½ cup (60 g) pastry flour
- 6 tablespoons (85 g) unsalted butter, cut into 6 pieces, at room temperature
- 3 large egg whites
- 2 tablespoons (30 g) whole-grain mustard
- 1 tablespoon (5 g) grated Parmesan cheese

SPECIAL EQUIPMENT

- Parchment paper
- Stand mixer

METHOD

Preheat the oven to 325°F (170°C, or gas mark 3). Line a sheet pan with parchment paper.

Spread the sliced olives on the lined sheet pan and dry them in the oven for 10 minutes. Set aside to cool. Transfer the olives to a small bowl and return the parchment to the pan.

Meanwhile, combine the flours and butter in the bowl of a stand mixer fitted with a paddle attachment. Beat on low speed for 3 minutes. The mixture will become crumbly and then form a smooth dough. Add the egg whites, mustard, and Parmesan cheese and mix for an additional 2 minutes, scraping the bowl and paddle as needed. Drop small scoops of batter, about 2 tablespoons (28 ml) each, on the parchment-lined pan. Spread each scoop of dough into a very thin circle. The circles do not have to be neat or exact in shape but should be evenly thin. Sprinkle the olives liberally over the circles and press gently so they adhere.

Bake for 10 minutes, rotate the pan, and bake just until the crisps are evenly golden and the edges are brown, 5 to 10 minutes more. Watch carefully so they do not get too dark. Cool the crisps on the pan for 1 minute and then transfer to a wire rack to cool completely. Repeat with the remaining batter and olives.

STORAGE

Store at room temperature in an airtight container for up to 1 day.

SILVER & GOLD

ACTIVE TIME: 5 MINUTES
TOTAL TIME: 5 MINUTES
SERVES: 1

INGREDIENTS

- 2 sheets silver and gold edible foil (see Ingredient Guide, page 217)
- 2 tablespoons (28 ml) chilled vodka
- 1 tablespoon (15 ml) Pineapple Shrub (below)
- ½ cup (120 ml) cold sparkling wine

THIS COCKTAIL TAKES JUST A MOMENT TO MIX, BUT THE MOST IMPORTANT INGREDIENT—THE SWEET AND SHARP PINEAPPLE SHRUB (BELOW)—NEEDS TO BE MADE TWO DAYS IN ADVANCE. (THE LEFTOVER PINEAPPLE PULP CAN BE PUREED AND USED AS JAM.) THE EDIBLE SILVER AND GOLD FOIL DOESN'T ADD FLAVOR; IT ADDS DRAMA AS IT DANCES IN THE CHAMPAGNE FLUTE.

METHOD

Crumble the edible foil into a champagne flute. Add the vodka and Pineapple Shrub and then the sparkling wine, pouring slowly to prevent it from bubbling over.

PINEAPPLE SHRUB

ACTIVE TIME: 20 MINUTES
TOTAL TIME: ABOUT 17 HOURS
YIELD: 2 CUPS (475 ML)

INGREDIENTS

- 1 pineapple, peeled, cored, and diced
- 1 cup (200 g) sugar
- ¼ cup (60 ml) champagne vinegar

SPECIAL EQUIPMENT

- Fine-mesh strainer

METHOD

Combine the pineapple and sugar in a large bowl and mix until the pineapple is evenly coated with sugar. Cover with plastic wrap and let sit at room temperature for about 8 hours. Stir until most of the sugar has dissolved and then add the vinegar. Cover the bowl and let sit for another 8 hours. Stir to make sure all the sugar is dissolved and then strain into a container with a tight-fitting lid.

STORAGE

Refrigerate in a tightly sealed container for up to 1 month.

TANIYA'S MACON MULE

ACTIVE TIME: 1 MINUTE
TOTAL TIME: 1 MINUTE
SERVES: 1

INGREDIENTS

- 3 tablespoons (45 ml) Maker's Mark or your favorite bourbon
- 1 tablespoon (15 ml) fresh lemon juice
- 1½ tablespoons (25 ml) Basil Peach Syrup (below)
- Ice cubes
- 6 tablespoons (90 ml) chilled ginger beer
- Peach wedge, for garnish
- Fresh basil leaves, for garnish

OUR FRIEND TANIYA NAYAK THROWS A GREAT PARTY. SHE'S AN INTERIOR DESIGNER, SO WE KNOW THE DECOR IS ALWAYS GOING TO BE SPOT-ON, BUT HER ATTENTION TO DETAIL DOESN'T STOP THERE. FOR A DERBY PARTY, SHE ASKED US TO CREATE A SIGNATURE COCKTAIL—A DRESSED-UP VERSION OF THE CLASSIC KENTUCKY MULE. WE TOOK THE RECIPE A LITTLE FURTHER SOUTH, ADDING GEORGIA PEACHES TO THE BOURBON AND GINGER BEER. (MAKE THE PEACH SYRUP A DAY IN ADVANCE.) TANIYA WOULD TELL YOU THIS IS BEST SERVED IN A TRADITIONAL COPPER MUG, GARNISHED WITH A PEACH WEDGE AND A SPRIG OF BASIL. WHO ARE WE TO ARGUE?

METHOD

In a 12-ounce (350 ml) glass, combine the bourbon, lemon juice, and Basil Peach Syrup. Fill the glass with ice and top with ginger beer; stir to combine. Garnish with a peach wedge and fresh basil leaves.

BASIL PEACH SYRUP

ACTIVE TIME: 20 MINUTES
TOTAL TIME: 8 TO 12 HOURS
YIELD: ABOUT 1½ CUPS (355 ML)

INGREDIENTS

- 3 peaches, peeled, pitted, and cut into chunks
- ½ cup (12 g) torn basil leaves
- 1 cup (200 g) sugar

SPECIAL EQUIPMENT

- Fine-mesh strainer

METHOD

Combine the peaches, basil, and sugar in a large bowl and mix until the peaches are evenly coated with sugar. Cover with plastic wrap and let sit at room temperature for 8 to 12 hours, stirring occasionally, until the sugar has dissolved and the peaches and basil are sitting in a pool of syrup. Strain the syrup into a container with a tight-fitting lid.

STORAGE

Refrigerate in a tightly sealed container for up to 2 weeks.

HOW TO DECORATE FOR A PARTY

Here are some tips from Taniya Nayak, celebrity interior designer and lifestyle expert.

CHOOSE A THEME.
A theme will help you make other decisions. Are you having a garden party (think about seasonal flowers) or a Moroccan-themed party (look for rich jewel tones)?

CONSIDER ALL THE ELEMENTS.
"You can break every party down into food, music, cocktail, attire, and design," Taniya says. "Each one of those is an opportunity to make your party memorable."

DON'T JUST DECORATE; REDECORATE.
Go ahead and move the furniture around. The arrangement that perfectly suits your day-to-day life is different from what works for a party. Create conversation nooks and different stations for food and drink throughout the space to keep the party flowing.

PLAN SOMETHING INTERACTIVE.
A mobile bar cart, a funny photo booth, a little craft project such as embellishing hats at a Kentucky Derby party—activities can jump-start conversations between guests.

DON'T OVERDO IT.
Decorating is about setting the stage for your guests, not overwhelming them. And you don't want to overwhelm yourself, either. The host should have fun, too.

CARAMELIZED BANANA PUDDING

ACTIVE TIME: 1 HOUR 20 MINUTES
TOTAL TIME: 5 HOURS 20 MINUTES
SERVES: 10 TO 12

INGREDIENTS

- 6 overripe bananas
- ¼ cup (48 g) turbinado sugar
- 4 cups plus 3 tablespoons (991 ml) whole milk, divided
- ½ cup (65 g) cornstarch
- ½ cup (34 g) instant nonfat dry milk
- ½ cup (100 g) granulated sugar
- 2 tablespoons (28 ml) vanilla extract
- 5 large egg yolks
- ½ cup (112 g) unsalted butter, chilled and cut into 5 pieces
- 1 cup (235 ml) heavy cream
- ¼ cup (30 g) confectioners' sugar
- ¼ cup (60 ml) sweetened condensed milk
- 1 box (11 ounces, or 310 g) of vanilla wafer cookies

SPECIAL EQUIPMENT

- Blender or food processor
- Fine-mesh strainer
- Electric mixer

EVERY TIME WILL GOES HOME TO FLORIDA, HIS MOM MAKES BANANA PUDDING. THE FAMILY RECIPE CALLS FOR JELL-O INSTANT PUDDING AND IT IS—WILL WOULD LIKE YOU TO KNOW—AMAZING. BUT HE COULDN'T RESIST CHEFFING IT UP A BIT WITH ROASTED BANANAS AND FROM-SCRATCH PUDDING. WILL ALWAYS EATS HIS MOM'S BANANA PUDDING RIGHT AWAY, BUT HE LIKES THIS VERSION BEST THE DAY AFTER IT IS MADE.

METHOD

Preheat your broiler. Line a sheet pan with aluminum foil.

Peel the bananas and place them in a bowl. Sprinkle with the turbinado sugar, turning to coat. Lay the bananas on the lined sheet pan and broil until the bananas are dark golden brown, about 5 minutes; watch carefully to avoid burning. Turn off the broiler and set the oven temperature to 500°F (250°C, or gas mark 10). Cook the bananas for 5 minutes more. Cool the bananas on the pan for 10 minutes and then transfer to a blender or food processor. Add 3 tablespoons (45 ml) of the milk, and process for 3 minutes; the puree should be thick and smooth. Transfer to a bowl and refrigerate until cool to the touch, about 45 minutes while you make the pudding.

Sift the cornstarch and dry milk powder into a medium bowl. Gradually whisk in 1 cup (235 ml) of milk, keeping the mixture smooth. Set aside.

Combine the remaining 3 cups (700 ml) milk, granulated sugar, and vanilla in a medium saucepan over medium-high heat.

Bring to a simmer, stirring occasionally, and whisk in the cornstarch mixture. Cook, stirring constantly, for 1 minute. The pudding should be thick and smooth. Remove from the heat.

Whisk in the egg yolks one at a time, stirring constantly to avoid scrambling. Whisk in the butter one piece at a time until thoroughly incorporated. Strain the pudding into a shallow bowl and press plastic wrap lightly on to the surface to prevent a skin from forming. Refrigerate until cold, about for 2 hours. Remove the banana puree from the refrigerator to return to room temperature while the pudding chills.

Combine the heavy cream and confectioners' sugar in a mixing bowl and use an electric mixer to beat until stiff peaks form. Add the sweetened condensed milk and beat again to incorporate.

Fold the banana puree into the pudding until evenly blended and then fold in the cream mixture. Cover loosely with plastic wrap and chill for at least 2 hours. The longer it chills, the better it is.

To assemble, spread a large spoonful of pudding in the bottom of a glass serving bowl. Cover the pudding with slightly

overlapping cookies and top with half the remaining pudding. Stand cookies around the perimeter of the bowl, facing out, and gently cover the surface of the pudding with more overlapping cookies. Top with the remaining pudding and garnish the top with some additional cookies.

STORAGE

Refrigerate the banana puree in a tightly sealed container for up to 3 days or freeze for up to 3 months. Refrigerate the pudding, covered with plastic wrap, for up to 4 days.

SAGAMORE RYE AND PEACH CLAFOUTI

ACTIVE TIME: 15 MINUTES
TOTAL TIME: 1 HOUR 15 MINUTES
SERVES: 8 TO 10

INGREDIENTS

- 4 peaches, peeled, pitted, and cut into 1-inch (2.5 cm) wedges (about 3¾ cups [578 g])
- ¼ cup (60 ml) Sagamore Spirit Straight Rye Whiskey
- ½ cup plus 1 tablespoon (113 g) granulated sugar, divided
- 1 cup (235 ml) whole milk
- 3 large eggs
- ½ cup (63 g) all-purpose flour
- ¼ cup (60 g) plain whole milk yogurt
- 2 tablespoons (28 g) unsalted butter, melted
- 1 teaspoon vanilla extract
- 1 teaspoon grated lemon zest
- ½ teaspoon kosher salt
- Confectioners' sugar, for garnish

SPECIAL EQUIPMENT

- Blender
- Nonstick spray

WHEN ANDY FIRST TASTED SAGAMORE SPIRIT STRAIGHT RYE WHISKEY AT THE DISTILLERY IN BALTIMORE, HE LIKED IT SO MUCH, HE BOUGHT A BARREL. (FOR THE RESTAURANT!) THE SWEETNESS AND CITRUS AND PEPPER NOTES OF THIS RYE ARE A PERFECT MATCH FOR SUMMER PEACHES IN THIS CLASSIC CLAFOUTI. (BUT HE'S SURE YOUR FAVORITE RYE WILL BE PRETTY GOOD, TOO.)

METHOD

Preheat the oven to 375°F (190°C, or gas mark 5).

Stir together the peaches, rye, and 1 tablespoon (13 g) of the sugar in a medium bowl. Set aside, stirring occasionally, while you prepare the batter.

Combine the remaining ½ cup (100 g) sugar, milk, eggs, flour, yogurt, melted butter, vanilla, lemon zest, and salt in a blender container and process for 1 minute. Set aside.

Generously grease the bottom and sides of a 9-inch (23 cm) pie or tart pan. (Try coating the pan with nonstick spray and then with butter for an easier release.) Spread the peaches and their liquid in the pan and pour the batter evenly over the top. (The pan will be very full.) Bake until the clafouti is puffed, set, and golden brown, 45 minutes to 1 hour.

Clafouti will be easier to cut into wedges if allowed to cool for at least 30 minutes. Dust with confectioners' sugar.

STORAGE

Store in a tightly covered for up to 2 days.

～～～～
TAIL GATE

A NDY'S BEEN TAILGATING AT PATRIOTS GAMES, WELL, BASICALLY FOREVER. THAT PREGAME GATHERING *MIGHT* EVEN BE MORE IMPORTANT TO HIM THAN THE FOOTBALL IT-SELF. BUT WILL HAS NEVER BEEN TO A TAILGATE; ANDY HAD TO TEACH HIM A FEW THINGS ABOUT THE ART OF TURNING A PARKING LOT INTO A PARTY.

The first step, if you're a chef: Invite the best cooks and bartenders you know. Andy's tailgate is a potluck and everybody brings their A game. There are bragging rights on the line. This is the time to fire up your famous hot wings (page 167) and make your own potato chips (page 178)—who's going to top that? Maybe Will. He's new to this, but he has a secret weapon: Pork Belly Burnt Ends (page 165), aka meat candy.

Some more tips from the pros: Choose dishes that can be made in advance or don't need much of your attention. Things that are good hot off the grill or at room temperature are winners, too. And definitely pack premixed cocktails. Andy will have a Frankie Fumbles Sazerac (page 180), thank you. You want great food and drink at your tailgate, but you also want time to toss around the football.

SALT AND PEPPER BABY BACKS

ACTIVE TIME: 30 MINUTES
TOTAL TIME: 2 HOURS
SERVES: 4 TO 6

INGREDIENTS

- ¼ cup (56 g) kosher salt
- ¼ cup (24 g) coarsely ground black pepper
- 1 tablespoon (9 g) garlic powder
- ½ teaspoon cayenne pepper
- 1 teaspoon dried rosemary leaves (optional)
- 2 racks baby back ribs (3 to 4 pounds [1.4 to 1.8 kg])
- Bare-Bones BBQ Sauce (page 35) or your favorite BBQ sauce, for serving

SPECIAL EQUIPMENT

- Charcoal grill
- Charcoal chimney
- Charcoal briquettes
- Instant-read thermometer

THE ONE AND ONLY DRAWBACK OF A TAILGATE: YOU MIGHT NOT ALWAYS HAVE A SMOKER AVAILABLE. THANKFULLY, YOU DON'T NEED ONE TO MAKE THESE AMAZING BABY BACKS. THEY AREN'T YOUR TRADITIONAL SMOKED RIBS. THINK OF THEM INSTEAD AS THE BEST GRILLED PORK CHOPS YOU'VE EVER TASTED, TENDER INSIDE WITH A CRUNCHY, SALTY EXTERIOR.

METHOD

Combine the salt, black pepper, garlic powder, cayenne pepper, and rosemary (if using) in a small bowl and mix well.

With a paper towel, peel the membrane off the bone side of the ribs. Evenly dust both sides of the ribs with the spice mix.

To prepare your charcoal grill for two-zone cooking, pile unlit charcoal against one side of the grill. Fill a charcoal chimney two-thirds full with briquettes to create medium-high heat. Stuff 2 sheets of newspaper into the bottom of the chimney and light the paper. When the coals are fully engaged—you should see flames peeking over the top—pour them over the unlit charcoal. When you can hold your hands 3 to 5 inches (7.5 to 13 cm) over the fire for no more than 3 to 5 seconds, clean the grill grate. Cover the grill and open the vents all the way. Wait 5 minutes.

Place the ribs on the cooler side of the grill, meat-side down. The closest rib should be 3 inches (7.5 cm) away from the hot coals. Keep all the vents completely open and place the cover back on the grill. Every 10 to 15 minutes, rotate the ribs, turning them over and end to end. You want to get a dark golden-brown crust on the ribs without burning them. Cook until the ribs reach an internal temperature of 170°F to 180°F (77°C to 82°C) when measured in the thickest part of the meat between the bones, about 1½ hours.

Serve with barbecue sauce.

STORAGE

Wrap room-temperature ribs tightly in plastic wrap. Refrigerate for up to 3 days or freeze for up to 1 month.

BIG BEEF RIB

ACTIVE TIME: 1 HOUR
TOTAL TIME: 7 HOURS
SERVES: 10 TO 12

INGREDIENTS

- 4 racks beef short ribs (about 5 pounds [2.3 kg] each)
- ¼ cup (60 ml) Worcestershire sauce
- ⅓ cup (50 g) Basic Beef BBQ Rub (page 32), divided
- ½ cup (120 ml) apple juice, as needed
- Your favorite barbecue sauce, for serving

SPECIAL EQUIPMENT

- Smoker and accessories (see page 212)
- Post oak or your favorite hardwood
- Probe thermometer
- Spray bottle
- Cooler, for holding meat

IF YOUR TAILGATE IS AS COMPETITIVE AS ANDY'S IS, THEN THIS IS THE DISH YOU WANT. THIS BEEF RIB SAYS, "ALL HAIL, THE KING HAS ARRIVED." EATING IT IS PRIMAL, PRIMITIVE. IT MAKES YOU FEEL LIKE FRED FLINTSTONE. THE SECRET IS A NICE SHORT RIB THAT ISN'T OVERTRIMMED. YOU WANT ABOUT ¼ INCH (6 MM) OF FAT SO THAT THE RIB BASTES ITSELF AS IT COOKS.

METHOD

Preheat your smoker to 250°F (121°C). About 30 minutes before you are ready to cook, stoke the fire with hardwood; we prefer post oak for this. (See page 212 for additional information on preparing a smoker.)

Trim as much silver skin as possible without losing too much of the meat. Paint the meaty tops of the ribs lightly with the Worcestershire sauce. The meat should look shiny, as if you were staining wood. Sprinkle evenly with all but a pinch of the rub. Let sit for 5 minutes and then knock off any excess rub.

Insert the thermometer probe in the smallest rib without letting it touch the bone and smoke the ribs to 192°F (89°C), about 4 hours. Pour the apple juice into a spray bottle. Once an hour, open the smoker and quickly mist the ribs with apple juice. When the ribs are done, remove them and wrap tightly in foil.

Prepare a tempered cooler by filling the cooler with warm water. Close the lid and wait 10 minutes. Remove the water, place the meat in the warm cooler, and close the lid. Allow the ribs to rest for 1 hour.

To serve, cut between each bone to separate the ribs. One at a time, flip the rib bone-side up and use the sharp point of a knife to slice through the thick membrane, down the middle of the bone. Twist out the bone and cut the cartilage off the sides of the meat. Carve the meat crosswise into ¼-inch (6 mm)-thick slices. Sprinkle the remaining rub on the meat before serving with your favorite barbecue sauce.

STORAGE

Refrigerate in a tightly sealed container for up to 4 days.

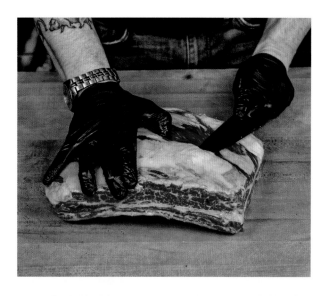

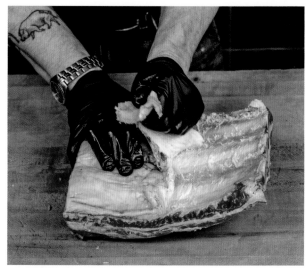

PORK BELLY BURNT ENDS

INGREDIENTS

- 1 gallon (3.8 L) water
- ½ cup (115 g) packed light brown sugar
- ½ cup (112 g) kosher salt
- 2 tablespoons (28 ml) fish sauce
- 1 tablespoon (6 g) cumin seeds, toasted
- 1 teaspoon fennel seeds
- 8 cloves garlic, smashed
- 2 teaspoons red pepper flakes
- 5 pounds (2.3 kg) pork belly, skin off
- 1¼ cups (188 g) Basic Pork BBQ Rub (page 32) or your favorite barbecue rub, divided
- 2 cups (475 ml) Smoky Hot BBQ Sauce (page 33) or your favorite barbecue sauce

SPECIAL EQUIPMENT

- Smoker and accessories (see page 212)
- Cherry wood or your favorite hardwood
- Probe thermometer

IT'S HARD TO BEAT SMOKED PORK BELLY. BUT WILL DID IT. HE SMOKES THESE BURNT ENDS TWICE, THE SECOND TIME TO CARAMELIZE THE SWEET-SALTY-SPICY GLAZE. THE RESULT IS BASICALLY MEAT CANDY. YOU CAN PACK WHATEVER IS LEFT AFTER THE PARTY BACK IN YOUR COOLER, BUT WE DON'T THINK THERE WILL BE ANY LEFTOVERS.

METHOD

Combine the water, brown sugar, salt, fish sauce, cumin seeds, fennel seeds, garlic, and red pepper flakes in a large pot over high heat and bring to a boil, stirring occasionally until the sugar and salt have dissolved. Remove from the heat, cool, and refrigerate overnight.

Place the pork belly in the chilled brine, cover, and refrigerate for 3 days, flipping every day.

Preheat your smoker to 275°F (135°C). About 30 minutes before you are ready to cook, stoke the fire with hardwood; we prefer cherry wood for this. (See page 212 for additional information on preparing a smoker.)

Remove the pork belly from the brine and pat dry. Lightly dust the pork all over with 1 cup (150 g) of the barbecue rub and insert the thermometer probe into the side of the meat. Smoke for 2 to 3 hours to an internal temperature of 180°F (82°C).

Remove from the smoker and allow to rest on a cutting board for 10 minutes. Cut into 1-inch (2.5 cm) cubes. Place the cubes on a wire rack and put the rack in the smoker for 1 hour more.

Meanwhile, in a small saucepan over medium heat, warm the barbecue sauce.

Remove the pork belly cubes from the smoker and toss in a large bowl with the warmed barbecue sauce and remaining ¼ cup (38 g) of barbecue rub. Toss to coat evenly. Spread the cubes on a baking sheet and return to the smoker for 45 minutes to 1¼ hours until the sauce is caramelized and sticky to the touch.

Remove from the smoker and cool for 15 minutes before serving.

STORAGE

Refrigerate in a tightly sealed container for up to 5 days.

THE SMOKE SHOP'S FAMOUS WINGS

ACTIVE TIME: 30 MINUTES

TOTAL TIME: 1 HOUR 30 MINUTES

SERVES: 10 TO 12 (48 PIECES)

INGREDIENTS

- 48 large chicken wing sections, drums and flats (5 to 6 pounds [2.3 to 2.7 kg])
- 1 cup (167 g) Not-So-Basic Chicken BBQ Rub, divided (page 32)
- 1 batch Agave Wing Seasoning (below) or Hot Wing Sauce (page 168)

SPECIAL EQUIPMENT

- Smoker and accessories (see page 212)
- Cherry wood, another fruitwood, or your favorite hardwood
- Instant-read thermometer

WE'VE BEEN MAKING THESE AT THE RESTAURANT SINCE OPENING DAY. PEOPLE ARE ALWAYS ASKING US WHAT THE SECRET IS, AND THEY ARE ALWAYS SURPRISED TO LEARN THAT THERE ISN'T ONE. YOU REALLY CAN'T MESS THIS UP. JUST CHOOSE MEATY WINGS FOR THIS—THE BIGGER, THE BETTER. THE ONLY HARD PART IS DECIDING BETWEEN THE SWEET AGAVE WING SEASONING AND THE SPICY HOT WING SAUCE.

METHOD

Preheat your smoker to 275°F (135°C). About 30 minutes before you are ready to cook, stoke the fire with hardwood; we prefer cherry wood or another fruitwood for this. (See page 212 for additional information on preparing a smoker.)

Place the wings in a large bowl, sprinkle evenly with the rub, and toss until evenly coated. Place the wings on the smoker rack, arranging them so they don't touch. (If possible, remove the smoker rack to arrange the wings.) Cook to an internal temperature of 165°F (74°C), about 1 hour.

Remove the wings from the smoker and place in a large bowl. Toss with the Agave Wing Seasoning or Hot Wing Sauce.

STORAGE

Refrigerate in a tightly sealed container for up to 3 days.

AGAVE WING SEASONING

ACTIVE TIME: 5 MINUTES

TOTAL TIME: 5 MINUTES

YIELD: ENOUGH TO COAT 48 PIECES OF CHICKEN

INGREDIENTS

- ⅓ cup (112 g) agave nectar
- ¼ cup (42 g) Not-So-Basic Chicken BBQ Rub (page 32)

METHOD

There's no real method here. Just toss the wings in the agave and then in the rub.

HOT WING SAUCE

ACTIVE TIME: 20 MINUTES
TOTAL TIME: 12 HOURS
YIELD: ABOUT 2 CUPS (475 ML)

INGREDIENTS

- 12 Fresno peppers, sliced into rings (about 2 cups [180 g])
- 8 large cloves garlic
- 1 cup (235 ml) apple cider vinegar
- ¼ cup (84 g) agave nectar
- ¼ cup (56 g) kosher salt
- ½ cup (112 g) unsalted butter, chilled and cut into pieces

SPECIAL EQUIPMENT

- Blender

METHOD

Combine the peppers and garlic in a heatproof bowl.

Bring the vinegar, agave nectar, and salt to boil in a small saucepan, stirring to blend; pour over the peppers and garlic. Allow to cool to room temperature and then cover with plastic wrap and let stand overnight at room temperature.

Transfer the mixture to a blender and process until well blended; it will not be completely smooth. Pour the puree into a medium saucepan and bring to a simmer. Whisk in the butter, once piece at a time, and then set aside to cool to room temperature. Return the mixture to the blender and process for 1 minute.

STORAGE

Refrigerate in a tightly sealed container for up to 1 week.

GARRETT'S TEX-MEX SHRIMP

ACTIVE TIME: 30 MINUTES
TOTAL TIME: 1 HOUR 30 MINUTES TO 2 HOURS 30 MINUTES PLUS OVERNIGHT CHILL
SERVES: 10 (30 TO 33 PIECES)

BOSTON RESTAURANT OWNER GARRETT HARKER IS ONE OF THE REGULARS AT ANDY'S PATRIOTS TAILGATE. HE RUNS ISLAND CREEK OYSTER BAR, THE CITY'S ALWAYS POPULAR OYSTER HOUSE, SO PEOPLE EXPECT HIM TO SERVE UP A KILLER SEAFOOD DISH AT THE GAMES. HE BROUGHT THIS ONE FOR A GAME AGAINST THE HOUSTON TEXANS. HIS ADVICE WHEN IT COMES TO TAILGATING: ALWAYS TAKE A RISK. "YOU DON'T WANT TO BE EATING THE SAME BORING STUFF EVERYONE ELSE IS," HE SAYS.

INGREDIENTS

- 3 limes
- ¼ cup (60 ml) grapeseed oil
- 1 tablespoon (5 g) coriander seeds, cracked
- 2 teaspoons kosher salt
- 2 teaspoons chili powder
- 1 teaspoon ground cumin
- 1 teaspoon red pepper flakes
- 1 bunch cilantro, leaves only, roughly chopped, divided
- 3 pounds (1.4 kg) extra-large (U-12) raw shrimp, peeled and deveined

SPECIAL EQUIPMENT

- Cooler
- Charcoal grill
- Charcoal chimney
- Charcoal briquettes

METHOD

The night before the big game, grate the lime zest into a large bowl. Add the oil, coriander, salt, chili powder, cumin, red pepper flakes, and half the cilantro to the lime zest, mix well, and refrigerate overnight. Quarter the zested limes and store them in a tightly sealed container.

Before you leave for the game, add the shrimp to the marinade, tossing until evenly coated. Transfer the shrimp and marinade to a tightly sealed container and pack in your cooler. Marinate the shrimp for 1 to 2 hours.

To build a hot direct fire in your grill, spread an even layer of unlit charcoal in the bottom of the grill. Fill a charcoal chimney two-thirds full with briquettes. Stuff 2 sheets of newspaper in the bottom of the chimney and light the paper. When the coals are fully engaged—you should see flames peeking over the top—pour them over the unlit charcoal.

When you can hold your hands 3 to 5 inches (7.5 to 13 cm) over the fire for no more than 3 to 5 seconds, clean the grill grate. Place the shrimp on the grate and grill for 3 to 5 minutes per side until golden brown and cooked through. The outer skin is pinkish red with a slight char on it and the split side has just turned from translucent to white.

Transfer the shrimp to a platter. Garnish with the reserved cilantro and drizzle with lime juice.

STORAGE

Refrigerate in a tightly sealed container for up to 4 days.

THE ULTIMATE BLT BAR

THERE IS ONE NONNEGOTIABLE IN THE ULTIMATE BLT: PERFECTLY RIPE TOMATOES. AFTER THAT, IT'S A CHOOSE YOUR OWN ADVENTURE SANDWICH. WILL YOU GO WITH THE CLASSIC MAPLE-SMOKED BACON (PAGE 172) OR THE HERBY MONEY MUSCLE COPPA (PAGE 174)? ANDY'S PERSONAL FAVORITE IS CAINS MAYONNAISE, BUT WILL YOU GO WITH THE LESS TRADITIONAL BASIL AIOLI (PAGE 177), SPICY MAYO (PAGE 177), OR WILL'S OUT-THERE SUGGESTION, BEER MUSTARD (PAGE 57)?

EVERYONE IS AN EXPERT ON BLT CONSTRUCTION: ANDY SAYS THE MAYO BELONGS ON BOTH PIECES OF BREAD AND THEN YOU PILE ON THE MEAT, LETTUCE, AND TOMATO, IN THAT ORDER. WILL THINKS THE MAYO BELONGS ON THE BOTTOM ONLY, THEN TOMATO, LETTUCE, AND MEAT. THANKFULLY, THEY BOTH AGREE ON THE HOMEMADE POTATO CHIPS (PAGE 178)—ON THE SIDE OR TUCKED INTO THE SANDWICH FOR A LITTLE EXTRA CRUNCH.

BLT BAR MENU

Maple-Smoked Bacon (page 172)	Mayonnaise
Money Muscle Coppa (page 174)	Basil Aioli (page 177)
Romaine lettuce	Spicy Mayo (page 177)
Sliced ripe tomatoes	Beer Mustard (page 57)
Sliced avocado	Homemade Potato Chips (page 178)
Sliced white bread	

MAPLE-SMOKED BACON

INGREDIENTS

- 3 sprigs fresh rosemary, leaves only (about ¼ cup [7 g])
- 2 tablespoons (28 g) kosher salt
- 2 tablespoons (15 g) chili powder
- 2 tablespoons (12 g) coarsely ground black pepper
- 2 tablespoons (28 ml) maple syrup
- 1 tablespoon (15 g) juniper berries, lightly crushed (see Ingredient Guide, page 217)
- Zest of 1 orange, minced
- 3 cloves garlic, roughly chopped
- ½ inch (1.3 cm) ginger, peeled and minced
- 1 teaspoon Prague powder, aka pink curing salt (see Ingredient Guide, page 217)
- ½ teaspoon ground nutmeg
- ¼ teaspoon ground allspice
- 2½ pounds (1.1 kg) skinless pork belly

SPECIAL EQUIPMENT

- Smoker and accessories (see page 212)
- Maple or your favorite hardwood
- Probe thermometer

METHOD

Combine all the seasonings in a small bowl and then rub the mixture evenly over the surface of the pork belly. Wrap the seasoned belly tightly in several layers of plastic wrap. Place it on a sheet pan and refrigerate for 3 days, flipping every day. On the third day, open the plastic wrap over the baking sheet and massage the cure into the meat again, spreading it evenly. Wrap the pork belly and all the juices tightly in several layers of plastic wrap and refrigerate for 2 days more, flipping each day.

Preheat your smoker to 200°F (93°C). About 30 minutes before you are ready to cook, stoke the fire with hardwood; we prefer maple for this. (See page 212 for additional information on preparing a smoker.)

Unwrap the pork belly, brushing off any large bits of cure such as rosemary leaves and juniper berries and place it on a wire rack set over a sheet pan. Let sit for 1 hour.

Insert the thermometer probe in the thickest part of the meat and smoke to an internal temperature of 165°F (74°C), 1 to 1½ hours. Leave the probe in place.

Transfer the meat to a sheet pan and refrigerate, uncovered, to an internal temperature of 40°F (4°C), at least 2 hours. Use a large, very sharp knife to cut the chilled meat into ¼-inch (6 mm)-thick slices.

When you are ready to serve, preheat the oven to 425°F (220°C, or gas mark 7). Lay the slices on a sheet pan and bake until hot and crisp, 5 to 7 minutes.

STORAGE

Wrap a piece of cardboard tightly with plastic wrap and shingle sliced, unbaked bacon on it. Wrap everything tightly in plastic wrap and freeze for up to 3 months.

MONEY MUSCLE COPPA

INGREDIENTS

- Money muscle from a 9- to 11-pound (4.1 to 5 kg) pork butt
- ¼ cup (60 ml) amaretto or Sambuca
- ¼ cup (60 g) packed light brown sugar
- 2 tablespoons (12 g) Italian seasoning, divided
- 1 tablespoon (14 g) kosher salt
- 1 tablespoon (6 g) coarsely ground black pepper
- 2 cloves garlic, minced
- 2 teaspoons juniper berries, slightly crushed (see Ingredient Guide, page 217)
- 1 teaspoon Prague powder, aka pink curing salt (see Ingredient Guide, page 217)
- 1 teaspoon cayenne pepper

SPECIAL EQUIPMENT

- Butcher's twine
- Smoker and accessories (see page 212)
- Hickory, oak, or your favorite hardwood
- Probe thermometer

METHOD

Trim the pork butt to isolate the money muscle. See page 176 for instructions or ask your butcher. Wrap the remaining pork butt tightly in plastic wrap and freeze for up to 3 months; it can be used for Classic Pulled Pork (page 18) or Sal's Boudin Balls (page 202).

Combine the seasoning ingredients in a small bowl, reserving 1 tablespoon (3 g) of the Italian seasoning. Mix into a paste.

Rub the surface of the money muscle well with the cure and wrap it tightly in plastic wrap. Set the package on a sheet pan and refrigerate for 3 days, flipping the meat every day.

Unwrap the money muscle, brushing off any large bits of cure such as juniper berries. Place the meat fat-side down on a work surface with a short end facing you. Sprinkle the remaining 1 tablespoon (3 g) of Italian seasoning evenly over the surface, and roll the meat up tightly, jelly-roll style, starting from the short side. Tie the roll at 1-inch (2.5 cm) intervals down the length of the roll with butcher's twine.

Preheat your smoker to 225°F (107°C). About 30 minutes before you are ready to cook, stoke the fire with hardwood; we prefer hickory or oak for this. (See page 212 for additional information on preparing a smoker.)

Insert the thermometer probe into the money muscle and smoke to an internal temperature of 170° (77°C), about 1½ hours. Cool to room temperature and then refrigerate overnight.

Preheat the oven to 425°F (220°C, or gas mark 7).

With a sharp slicer knife, remove the twine and slice the money muscle crosswise into ⅛-inch (3 mm)-thick slices. Place on a wire rack set over a sheet pan and bake until crispy and starting to brown, 7 to 10 minutes.

STORAGE

Wrap a piece of cardboard tightly with plastic wrap and shingle sliced, unbaked coppa on it. Wrap everything tightly in plastic wrap and freeze for up to 3 months.

WHAT THE BUTCHER KNOWS:

MONEY MUSCLE

WHAT IT IS: It's a portion of the pork butt, a well-marbled cylinder of meat running along the rib section of the pig.

WHAT TO ASK FOR: Most butchers will know it as coppa (the name given to the Italian cured meat made from the muscle). It is carved from the pork butt, NAMP #406.

WHY TO CHOOSE IT: "It's the very best part of the pork butt," Ronnie says. "It has great flavor and is the most tender cut."

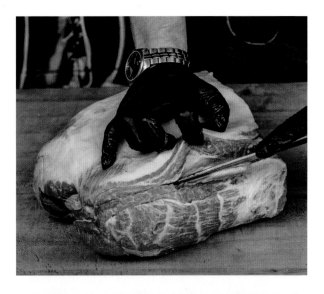

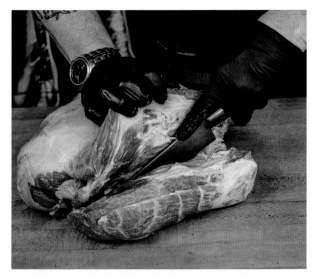

BASIL AIOLI

INGREDIENTS

- 1 cup (24 g) loosely packed basil leaves, divided
- 2 large eggs
- 2 tablespoons (28 ml) fresh lemon juice
- 4 cloves garlic, smashed
- 1 tablespoon (15 g) Dijon mustard
- 2 cups (475 ml) vegetable oil
- 1 teaspoon kosher salt
- ½ teaspoon coarsely ground pepper

SPECIAL EQUIPMENT

- Food processor or blender

METHOD

Combine ½ cup (12 g) of the basil leaves, the eggs, lemon juice, garlic, and mustard in a food processor or blender; purée. With the machine running, slowly drizzle in the oil until the mixture is smooth, thick, and shiny. Add the remaining ½ cup (12 g) of basil and pulse. Season with salt and pepper. Refrigerate until needed.

STORAGE

Refrigerate in a tightly sealed container for up to 1 week.

SPICY MAYO

INGREDIENTS

- 2 jalapeño or serrano peppers, roughly chopped
- ¼ cup (60 ml) white vinegar
- 2 large egg yolks
- 1 teaspoon Dijon mustard
- 1 teaspoon garlic powder
- 1 teaspoon kosher salt
- ½ teaspoon Worcestershire sauce
- 2 cups (475 ml) vegetable oil
- 1 teaspoon flaky sea salt

SPECIAL EQUIPMENT

- Food processor or blender

METHOD

Combine the peppers, vinegar, egg yolks, mustard, garlic powder, kosher salt, and Worcestershire sauce in a food processor or blender and purée until the peppers are finely chopped. With the machine running, slowly drizzle in the oil until the mixture is smooth, thick, and shiny. Pulse in the flaky salt. Refrigerate until needed.

STORAGE

Refrigerate in a tightly sealed container for up to 1 week.

HOMEMADE POTATO CHIPS

ACTIVE TIME: 20 MINUTES
TOTAL TIME: 30 MINUTES
SERVES: 10 TO 12

SURE, YOU COULD JUST BUY POTATO CHIPS, BUT YOU'LL WIN THE TAILGATE WITH THESE HOMEMADE CRISPS. FRY THE POTATOES THE DAY BEFORE, BUT WAIT TO COAT THEM IN RANCH DUST (BELOW) OR YOUR FAVORITE BBQ RUB AT THE PARTY—SIMPLY BECAUSE IT'S A MOMENT THAT WOWS EVERYONE. YOU CAN'T OVERSEASON THESE.

INGREDIENTS

- 4 pounds (1.8 kg) russet potatoes
- ¼ cup (60 ml) white vinegar
- About 12 cups (2.8 L) vegetable oil
- 1 batch Ranch Dust (optional; below)

SPECIAL EQUIPMENT

- Deep-fry thermometer

METHOD

Slice the potatoes as thinly as possible. (For best results, use a mandoline to slice the potatoes into 1/16-inch [2 mm] pieces.)

Rinse the sliced potatoes in batches until the starch is removed and the water runs clear. Place all the potatoes in a large bowl and cover with water. Add the vinegar and set aside until you are ready to fry, up to 1 hour.

Attach a deep-fry thermometer to the side of a deep heavy-bottomed pan. Pour the oil in to a depth of 3 inches (7.5 cm) and place the pan over medium-high heat. (You want to try to maintain this temperature.)

Drain the potatoes and pat very dry. When the oil reaches 325°F to 350°F (170°C to 180°C), fry the potatoes in batches. Use a slotted spoon to gently move the potato chips around. Flip the chips after 2 to 3 minutes. The chips are done when they are evenly deep golden brown, 2 to 3 minutes on each side.

Transfer the chips to a paper towel–lined sheet pan to drain and toss with the Ranch Dust, if using.

STORAGE

Store at room temperature in an airtight container for up to 2 days.

RANCH DUST

ACTIVE TIME: 10 MINUTES
TOTAL TIME: 10 MINUTES
YIELD: ABOUT 1⅓ CUPS (126 G)

INGREDIENTS

- ¾ cup (90 g) dry buttermilk powder
- 3 tablespoons (4 g) dried parsley
- 1 tablespoon dried chives
- 1 tablespoon plus 2 teaspoons (5 g) dried dill
- 1 tablespoon (9 g) garlic powder
- 1 tablespoon (7 g) onion power
- 1 tablespoon (10 g) garlic flakes
- 1 tablespoon (5 g) onion flakes
- 2 teaspoons kosher salt
- 1½ teaspoons coarsely ground black pepper
- 1 teaspoon chili powder

SPECIAL EQUIPMENT

- Food processor

METHOD

Combine all the ingredients in a food processor and pulse for 30 seconds.

STORAGE

Store in a cool, dark place in an airtight container for up to several months.

FRANKIE FUMBLES SAZERAC

ACTIVE TIME: 25 MINUTES

TOTAL TIME: 25 MINUTES
PLUS 12 HOURS

SERVES: 12 TO 14

CREDIT FOR THIS COCKTAIL GOES TO FRANK REARDON, ONE OF THOSE BARTENDERS WHO ALWAYS REMEMBERS YOUR NAME AND YOUR DRINK. THIS IS ANDY'S GO-TO AT TAILGATES, BUT IT CAN ALSO BE HIS UNDOING. IT'S A LOT STRONGER THAN IT TASTES! THIS IS THE PERFECT CONCOCTION FOR A PARKING-LOT PARTY BECAUSE EVERYTHING IS MADE AND MIXED IN ADVANCE. AND IT'S JUST AS GOOD FROM PLASTIC CUPS AS IT IS FROM CRYSTAL ROCKS GLASSES.

INGREDIENTS

- 1 lemon
- 2 tablespoons (28 ml) vegetable oil
- 6 tablespoons (90 ml) water
- 6 tablespoons (72 g) Demerara sugar
- 750 ml bottle Bulleit rye
- 1 tablespoon (15 ml) Peychaud's bitters
- 2 tablespoons (28 ml) absinthe

SPECIAL EQUIPMENT

- Fine-mesh strainer

METHOD

To make the lemon oil, use a vegetable peeler to remove the lemon zest in long swaths. Place the zest in a small saucepan and reserve the lemon for another use. Add the oil to the pan and bring to a gentle simmer over medium heat. Cook for 10 minutes; the zest will shrink and release its own oils. Set aside to cool. Strain the oil into a tightly sealed container and refrigerate for up to 2 weeks.

To make the Demerara simple syrup, combine the water and sugar in a small saucepan over medium heat. Bring to a simmer, stirring to dissolve. Cook for 2 minutes and then cool. Transfer the syrup to a tightly sealed container and refrigerate until needed.

Combine the rye, bitters, and ½ cup (120 ml) of Demerara simple syrup in a 1½-quart (1.4 L) pitcher, reserving the rye bottle. Mix well and then carefully pour or funnel the batched cocktail back into the empty bottle. (There will be a little left over; you can drink that to "test" it.) Seal the bottle and refrigerate overnight, keeping the bottle super cold until the game.

Pour the absinthe into a cup, swirl it around, and then pour it into the next cup. Repeat for each drink with the same 2 tablespoons (28 ml) of absinthe. Discard (or drink) any absinthe that remains after each cup is coated. Measure 6 tablespoons (90 ml) of the pre-batched cocktail into each cup and garnish with about ⅛ teaspoon lemon oil.

HOW TO PICK WINES FOR A TAILGATE

Here are some tips from Garrett Harker, wine guy and tailgate regular.

FORGET ABOUT BEER.
Wine is a natural for pairing with food. Beaujolais and Riesling are two of Garrett's go-tos for game days. They are flexible enough to complement a Big Beef Rib (page 162) or a BLT (page 170).

DO SOMETHING DRAMATIC.
"You can't go wrong with bubbles, even if you are just standing around in a parking lot in a Pats jersey," Garrett says. He likes to bring Cava or Prosecco in magnums (twice the size of a typical bottle). It just looks cooler.

PLAN FOR THE WHOLE SEASON.
Rosé is a favorite in September when everyone is still thinking about summer. By December, Garrett is warming up with Syrah, a red that goes great with smoke, and Spanish reds aged in American oak, which are a surprisingly good with seafood.

DON'T BE AFRAID OF A RED SOLO CUP.
"I'd be lying if I told you I haven't had great wine out of a Solo cup," Garrett says. "I have, and I'm proud of it." But he's also a fan of disposable wineglasses or if he's bringing something special, stemless Riedel glasses. "Yes, people look at us like we're crazy," he says. That's part of the fun.

DERBY SLAB BARS

ACTIVE TIME: 30 MINUTES
TOTAL TIME: 6 HOURS
SERVES: 12 TO 16

THIS IS SARAH'S SIGNATURE DESSERT. IT'S BASICALLY PECAN PIE, IMPROVED. THE CRUST IS FLAKY, A BIT LIKE SHORTCAKE. (THE TRICK IS TO KEEP EVERYTHING AS COLD AS POSSIBLE WHEN YOU ARE MIXING THE DOUGH.) AND THE COMBINATION OF MAPLE AND BOURBON JUST MAKES SO MUCH SENSE.

INGREDIENTS

CRUST

- 2½ cups (320 g) all-purpose flour
- 2¼ tablespoons (29 g) sugar
- 1½ tablespoons (14 g) cornmeal
- 1¼ teaspoons kosher salt
- 18 tablespoons (252 g) cold salted butter, cut into ¼-inch (6 mm) pieces
- 10 tablespoons (125 g) vegetable shortening, frozen and cut into large cubes
- 4 to 6 tablespoons (60 to 90 ml) ice water

FILLING

- 3½ cups (700 g) sugar
- 1¼ cups (280 g) salted butter, cut into 10 pieces, softened
- 5 large eggs
- ½ cup (120 ml) bourbon
- 6 tablespoons (47 g) all-purpose flour
- 3 tablespoons (60 ml) maple syrup
- ¾ teaspoon kosher salt
- 2½ cups (438 g) chocolate chips
- 2 cups (220 g) chopped pecans

SPECIAL EQUIPMENT

- Food processor
- Parchment paper
- Blender

METHOD

To make the crust, combine the flour, sugar, cornmeal, and salt in the bowl of a food processor and pulse to blend. Add the butter, pulsing once to lightly cover the pieces with flour, and then pulse to combine in five 1-second pulses. Add the shortening and pulse 10 to 12 more times until the dough looks like very coarse meal with some large chunks. Add 4 tablespoons (60 ml) of the ice water and process until it starts to clump. You should still be able to see bits of fat in the flour. If the dough is dry, pulse in up to 2 tablespoons (28 ml) more water, 1 teaspoon at a time, being careful not to overmix.

Place two 18-inch (46 cm)-long pieces of plastic wrap on your work surface, overlapping to form a plus sign. Gather the dough in the center of the plastic and shape it into a 5 × 7-inch (13 × 18 cm) rectangle that is about 1 inch (2.5 cm) thick. Wrap securely in the plastic wrap and refrigerate until firm, at least 3 hours.

Place the dough on a well-floured, 20 × 15-inch (51 × 38 cm) sheet of parchment paper. Roll the dough to a 19 × 14-inch (48 × 36 cm) rectangle. Use the parchment to carefully turn the dough out into a 19 × 14-inch (48 × 36 cm) sheet pan, making sure it is centered. Carefully peel off and discard the parchment. Press the dough into the corners thoroughly and up the sides of the pan, leaving a ¼- to ½-inch (6 to 13 mm) overhang. Wrap any excess dough in plastic wrap and refrigerate it; you will need it to fill in any cracks in the baked crust. Crimp the edge of the dough in whatever decorative manner you like. Use a fork to prick the bottom of the crust all over, leaving no more than ¾ inch (2 cm) of space between holes. Place the pan in the freezer for at least 20 minutes. Cover the crust in 2 layers of aluminum foil, carefully pressing it into the corners and around the crimped edge. Use a fork to prick through the foil 25 to 30 times, about every 2 inches (5 cm). Freeze again for 10 minutes.

While the crust is in the freezer, preheat the oven to 400°F (200°C, or gas mark 6) and place an inverted sheet pan on the center rack.

Position the frozen crust pan on top of the inverted pan and bake until completely set, 20 to 25 minutes. Remove the foil carefully to avoid breaking the edge of the crust and bake for another 3 to 7 minutes until it looks dry but not brown. Remove the crust from the oven, leaving the inverted pan in place. Place on a wire rack and immediately fill any holes or cracks with the reserved dough trimmings, pressing and smoothing in place. This will prevent the filling from

leaking through and sticking to the sheet pan. Cool for at least 15 minutes.

Lower the oven temperature to 375°F (190°C, or gas mark 5). Keep the inverted pan in the oven.

To make the filling, combine the sugar, butter, eggs, bourbon, flour, maple syrup, and salt in a blender and process until thoroughly combined and uniform in color, about 2 minutes.

Scatter the chocolate chips and pecans over the crust and then pour the egg-butter mixture over them, covering them thoroughly.

Place on top of the inverted sheet pan in the oven and bake for 25 minutes. Then remove the inverted sheet pan and continue cooking, if necessary, until the top is golden brown and the filling is set but still jiggles, 20 to 25 minutes more. Transfer to a wire rack to cool for 30 to 45 minutes before cutting into squares.

STORAGE

Store at room temperature in an airtight container for up to 5 days.

THE HOLIDAY
PARTY

YOU DON'T NEED AN EXCUSE TO THROW A PARTY. WE HOPE WE'VE PROVEN THAT TO YOU WITH THIS BOOK. YOU SHOULD THROW A SHINDIG ON A SUMMERY SATURDAY AFTERNOON SIMPLY BECAUSE THERE'S A BRISKET IN THE SMOKER, AND TACOS ARE MORE THAN ENOUGH REASON CELEBRATE ON A TUESDAY NIGHT. (WE'LL BE LOOKING FOR OUR INVITE.) BUT THE HOLIDAYS—THEY ARE THE CHERRY ON TOP FOR THE PARTY PLANNER. THERE'S ALREADY EXCITEMENT IN THE AIR AND PEOPLE ARE HUNGRY FOR FOOD, FRIENDS, AND FUN.

For the cook, the holidays can be a time to go over the top, perhaps with an elaborate Crown Roast of Pork (page 186) or caviar. (It won't surprise you that we forgo the blini for BBQ chips.) But the season can also be a time to stick to tradition. For Will, that's Hoppin' John (page 204), which his family has every New Year's Day, while Andy just loves the hodgepodge of a holiday party. It's a feast that can incorporate everyone's food memories, whether you've always celebrated with a glazed ham (page 189) or take-out Chinese food (DIY with Brisket Fried Rice, page 192).

And, of course, you can make your own traditions. At Andy's house, that's the Make Your Own 'Nog (page 210). His guests all know they can toast the holidays with friends—and a taste of Andy's vast bourbon collection.

CROWN ROAST OF PORK

ACTIVE TIME: 45 MINUTES

TOTAL TIME: 16 HOURS

SERVES: 10 TO 12

INGREDIENTS

- ¼ cup (56 g) kosher salt
- 2 tablespoons (12 g) coarsely ground black pepper
- 2 tablespoons (5 g) chopped fresh sage leaves
- 2 tablespoons (5 g) fresh thyme leaves
- 5 tablespoons (75 ml) extra virgin olive oil, divided
- 2 tablespoons (22 g) yellow mustard
- 7 cloves garlic, divided
- 6- to 10-pound (2.7 to 4.6 kg) crown roast of pork (trimmings reserved)
- 2 large shallots, roughly chopped (about ¾ cup [120 g])
- 1 medium carrot, peeled and sliced ½-inch (1.3 cm) thick (about ½ cup [61 g])
- 2 stalks celery, diced
- 2 sprigs fresh thyme
- 2 sprigs fresh sage
- 3 tablespoons (48 g) tomato paste
- 1 cup (235 ml) red wine
- 6 cups (1.4 L) chicken broth

SPECIAL EQUIPMENT

- Food processor
- Smoker and accessories (see page 217)
- Maple, oak, or your favorite hardwood
- Probe thermometer
- Fine-mesh strainer

THERE MIGHT BE NOTHING MORE IMPRESSIVE THAN A CROWN ROAST SITTING IN THE MIDDLE OF YOUR HOLIDAY TABLE. (THERE'S NO REASON TO TELL ANYONE THAT YOUR BUTCHER DID MOST OF THE HARD WORK OF COAXING THE RIBS INTO THEIR REGAL SHAPE.) AND EVERYONE LOVES A PORK CHOP, ESPECIALLY ONE BATHED IN SMOKED JUS. WILL CALLS THIS DISH THE GIFT THAT KEEPS ON GIVING: THE LEFTOVERS MAKE AMAZING SANDWICHES.

METHOD

In a food processor, combine the salt, pepper, chopped herbs, 2 tablespoons (28 ml) of the olive oil, mustard, and 3 of the garlic cloves and pulse until well blended.

Place the crown roast on a sheet pan. Spread a thin layer of the seasoning mixture all over the meat, wrap the crown roast loosely with plastic wrap, and refrigerate for 12 hours.

Remove the roast from the refrigerate 1 hour before you intend to smoke it. This will ensure a faster cook time. Wrap each exposed bone with a square of foil to cover.

Preheat your smoker to 300°F (150°C). About 30 minutes before you are ready to cook, stoke the fire with hardwood; we prefer maple or oak for this. (See page 212 for additional information on preparing a smoker.)

Smash the remaining 4 garlic cloves and place in a baking pan along with the pork trimmings, shallots, carrot, celery, herbs sprigs, tomato paste, and remaining 3 tablespoons (45 ml) of olive oil. Stir to coat with the oil. Place a thermometer probe in the thickest part of the meat. Place the roast in the center of the smoker and put a baking pan underneath the roast to catch the drippings. Smoke to 150°F (66°C), about 2 hours.

Remove the meat from the smoker and remove the foil and the twine. Let rest for 15 minutes while you remove the baking pan with the drippings from the smoker. Place the baking pan over medium-high heat and add the wine. Bring to a boil, scraping any caramelized pieces from the bottom of the pan. Transfer the contents to a medium saucepan and boil for 2 minutes. Add the chicken broth and adjust the heat to simmer for 40 minutes. Strain the jus and keep it warm.

CONTINUED

To carve the roast, transfer it to the cutting board. Divide the roast into two semicircles. Turn the bone side toward you. Start by placing your knife between the two bones at either end. With your free hand, hold the top of the bones and gently slice downward. If you hit bone, do not panic, just use the bone as a guide to finish slicing. Continue this until all the chops have been sliced. Serve with a gravy boat filled with jus.

STORAGE

Refrigerate the wet rub in a tightly sealed container for up to 5 days. Refrigerate the jus in a tightly sealed container for up to 5 days. Wrap any leftover meat tightly in plastic wrap and refrigerate for up to 5 days or freeze for up to 3 months.

WHAT THE
BUTCHER
KNOWS:

CROWN ROAST OF PORK

WHAT IT IS: It's the rib section of the pig, curled into a ring and the bones frenched.

WHAT TO ASK FOR: Ask for it by name or number, NAMP #412G. (It can be difficult to shape fewer than 16 ribs into a crown, so if you aren't feeding a crowd, you could ask for a stockade—two interlocking racks of ribs—which is more flexible in size, but similarly impressive.)

WHY TO CHOOSE IT: "It's a delicious tradition," Ronnie says. And don't overlook the meat and fat removed when the butcher frenches the bones. It's great in a jus or—Ronnie's favorite—ground and added to stuffing.

BROWN SUGAR HAM WITH PRETZEL BUNS

ACTIVE TIME: 10 MINUTES
TOTAL TIME: 3 TO 4 HOURS
SERVES: 12

YOU COULD SMOKE YOUR OWN HAM (PAGE 53), BUT EVERYONE WILL BE PAYING ATTENTION TO THE GLAZE HERE. FOR THE TRADITIONALISTS, THIS IS BASICALLY HONEY-BAKED HAM—BUT BETTER, BATHED IN BROWN SUGAR, BOURBON, AND WARM SPICES. SLICE IT THIN AND SERVE IT ON PRETZEL BUNS (PAGE 191). THEY DON'T TAKE MUCH MORE TIME THAN A DINNER ROLL, AND THEY ADD A LITTLE PIZZAZZ TO ANY PARTY.

INGREDIENTS

- 10- to 12-pound (4.6 to 5.5 kg) cooked ham
- 1 cup (225 g) packed light brown sugar
- ½ cup (120 ml) bourbon or rye
- ½ cup (170 g) honey
- Grated zest of 1 orange
- ½ teaspoon ground cloves
- 1 clove garlic, minced
- ⅓-inch (8 mm) piece ginger, peeled and minced
- 1 teaspoon ground cinnamon
- ½ teaspoon coarsely ground black pepper
- 1 batch Pretzel Buns (page 191), for serving

METHOD

Preheat the oven to 325°F (170°C, or gas mark 3).

Score the rounded side of the ham about ¼ inch (6 mm) deep in a diamond pattern. Place the ham cut-side down on a rack in a baking pan just large enough to hold it and add ½ cup (120 ml) of water to the pan. Bake according to package directions, to 145°F (63°C), 15 to 20 minutes per pound.

Combine the brown sugar, bourbon, honey, orange zest, and spices in a medium saucepan. Bring to a simmer and cook, stirring to dissolve the sugar, for 5 minutes. Set aside until needed.

About 30 minutes before the ham is done, remove it from the oven. Increase the oven temperature to 375°F (190°C, or gas mark 5). If the water in the pan has evaporated, add another ½ cup (120 ml). Brush or pour the glaze over the top of the ham and return it to the oven for the last half hour of cooking.

Slice thinly and serve with Pretzel Buns.

STORAGE

Cool the glaze to room temperature and refrigerate in a tightly sealed container for up to 1 week. Refrigerate glazed ham in a tightly sealed container for up to 1 month.

PRETZEL BUNS

ACTIVE TIME: 40 MINUTES
TOTAL TIME: 3 HOURS 30 MINUTES
YIELD: 12 PIECES

INGREDIENTS

- 3 cups (360 g) bread flour
- 1⅓ cups (160 g) pastry flour
- 1¾ cups (410 ml) warm water
- 2 teaspoons molasses
- 1 teaspoon sugar
- 1 teaspoon instant dry yeast
- ¼ cup (60 ml) warm milk
- 3 tablespoons (42 g) unsalted butter, cut into 6 pieces
- ¼ cup (55 g) baking soda
- 2 teaspoons kosher salt
- ¼ cup (60 g) flaky sea salt or pretzel salt

SPECIAL EQUIPMENT

- Stand mixer

METHOD

Sift the bread flour and the pastry flour into the bowl of a stand mixer fitted with a hook attachment.

Stir together the warm water, molasses, and sugar in a medium bowl. Sprinkle the yeast over the mixture and proof for 5 minutes. Stir in the milk. Add the liquid to the flour and mix on medium speed until a sticky dough ball forms, about 5 minutes. While mixing, add the butter one piece at a time. The dough should be smooth and slightly sticky.

Grease a bowl with some oil and transfer the dough to the bowl, cover with a towel, and let rise in a warm place until the dough has doubled in size, about 1 hour.

Grease your work surface and a sheet pan with some oil.

Gently press on the dough to deflate and turn it out onto the greased work surface. Divide it into 12 equal pieces and shape into smooth, 3-ounce (85 g) balls. Arrange the balls on the greased sheet pan as you form them, keeping them loosely covered to prevent crusting. Let them rise again, loosely covered, for 15 minutes.

Preheat the oven to 400°F (200°C, or gas mark 6).

While the dough is rising, dissolve the baking soda and kosher salt in 4 cups (946 ml) of warm water in a shallow bowl. Dunk each ball of dough into the soda water and return it to the sheet pan. While they are still wet, sprinkle each with a bit of the flaky salt and use a sharp paring knife to slash a ½-inch (1.3 cm) deep cross on the tops.

Transfer the sheet pan to the oven and bake until the rolls are dark golden brown, about 25 minutes; be careful not to burn the bottoms. Transfer to a wire rack to cool completely.

STORAGE

Cool the baked buns completely and store at room temperature in an airtight container for up to 3 days.

BRISKET FRIED RICE

ACTIVE TIME: 1 HOUR
TOTAL TIME: 1 HOUR PLUS OVERNIGHT
SERVES: 12 TO 15

INGREDIENTS

- 2 cups (360 g) uncooked jasmine rice
- 2¼ cups (535 g) water
- 1 teaspoon kosher salt
- 2 tablespoons (28 ml) vegetable oil, divided
- 1 tablespoon (15 ml) sesame oil
- 16 ounces (455 g) Kinda Simple Beef Brisket (page 24), diced
- 1-inch (2.5 cm) piece ginger, peeled and minced (about 1 tablespoon [6 g])
- 2 cloves garlic, minced
- 1 large yellow onion, diced (about 3 cups [480 g])
- 2 stalks celery, diced (about ⅔ cup [80 g])
- 1 large carrot, peeled and diced
- 1 small head bok choy, cut crosswise into ¼-inch (6 mm) strips (4 to 5 cups [280 to 350 g])
- 1 cup (145 g) fresh or (130 g) thawed frozen peas, blanched
- ¼ cup (60 ml) fish sauce
- ¼ cup (60 ml) soy sauce
- ¼ cup (60 g) sambal olek
- ¼ cup (4 g) roughly chopped cilantro, divided
- ¼ cup (10 g) roughly chopped basil, divided
- ¼ cup (24 g) roughly chopped mint, divided
- 4 large eggs

SPECIAL EQUIPMENT

- Fine-mesh strainer

FRIED RICE IS A GREAT WAY TO USE UP LEFTOVERS. NO ONE WILL EVER NOTICE YOUR SLEIGHT OF HAND. THEY'LL BE TOO BUSY OOHING AND AHHING OVER THE FLAVORFUL RICE. AT THE SMOKE SHOP, THERE'S ALWAYS A LEFTOVER BIT OF BRISKET, SO THAT'S THE CENTERPIECE OF THIS VERSION. THE REAL STAR, THOUGH, IS THE EGG. STIR IT INTO THE HOT RICE IN FRONT OF YOUR GUESTS FOR ADDED DRAMA AND PERFECTLY CREAMY RICE.

METHOD

Place the jasmine rice in a fine-mesh strainer and rinse until the water runs clear; drain well. Combine the rice, water, and salt in a 2-quart (1.9 L) saucepan over medium-high heat. Bring to a boil, stir well, and lower the heat to a simmer; cook, partly covered, until the rice is tender, about 18 minutes. Set aside to cool and then transfer to a container with a tight-fitting lid and refrigerate overnight.

Heat 1 tablespoon (15 ml) of the vegetable oil and the sesame oil in a large heavy-bottomed pan over medium-high heat. (Unless your pan in enormous, it's best to make this in two batches, using half of the ingredients in each.) When the oil is smoking hot, add the brisket, ginger, and garlic and cook, stirring, until fragrant, about for 1 minute.

Add the onion, celery, and carrot and continue to cook and stir until the vegetables just start to soften and brown slightly, 1 to 2 minutes. Add the bok choy and peas; continue to cook, stirring continually and scraping up any browned bits stuck to the pan, until the peas are hot and the bok choy is starting to wilt, 1 to 2 minutes.

Increase the heat to medium-high and add the rice. Cook, stirring to break it up, for about 2 minutes and then add the fish sauce, soy sauce, and sambal oelek. Give it a good stir and taste for seasoning (you might want a little more soy or sambal). Remove from the heat and fold in half of the fresh herbs. Transfer the fried rice to a shallow serving bowl and use the back of a large spoon to make a shallow well in the rice to hold the eggs.

Add the remaining 1 tablespoon (15 ml) of vegetable oil to a medium nonstick sauté pan over medium-high heat. While the pan is heating, break the eggs into a bowl. Swirl the oil around the hot pan and gently pour in the eggs without breaking the yolks. When the egg whites start to set, nudge the eggs with a plastic spatula to make sure they do not stick. Continue to cook the eggs "sunny side up" until the whites are opaque but the yolks are not set. Carefully slide the eggs onto the fried rice. Garnish with the remaining chopped herbs and rush the bowl to the table.

Quickly, use a chopstick or fork to stir the eggs into the hot rice, where they will continue to cook and make the rice creamy.

STORAGE

Refrigerate in a tightly sealed container for up to 4 days.

SMOKED FISH DIP

ACTIVE TIME: 40 MINUTES

TOTAL TIME: 4 HOURS 30 MINUTES
TO 5 HOURS 30 MINUTES

SERVES: 10 TO 12

INGREDIENTS

- 4 cups (946 ml) water
- ½ cup (112 g) plus 1 teaspoon kosher salt, divided
- ¼ cup (50 g) sugar
- 8 ounces (225 g) cod or hake fillet
- 1 cup (230 g) Greek yogurt
- 1 cup (230 g) sour cream
- 2 medium shallots, minced (about 6 tablespoons [56 g])
- 2 teaspoons coarsely ground black pepper
- 1 teaspoon Old Bay Seasoning
- Asiago Black Pepper Crackers (page 196), for serving

SPECIAL EQUIPMENT

- Smoker and accessories (see page 217)
- Alder, oak, or your favorite hardwood
- Probe thermometer

HISTORICALLY, SMOKED AND CURED FISH DISHES WERE A STAPLE OF THE NEW ENGLAND WINTER HOLIDAYS. THE FISHERMEN WEREN'T GOING OUT IN *THAT* WEATHER. NOW, YOU CAN GET GREAT FISH YEAR-ROUND, BUT WHEN THE DAYS ARE SHORT, YOU'LL STILL GET A CRAVING FOR THIS RICH, SMOKY FISH DIP. SERVE THIS ONE WITH ASIAGO BLACK PEPPER CRACKERS—BASICALLY A FANCY VERSION OF GOLDFISH CRACKERS.

METHOD

Bring the water to a boil in a small saucepan. Add ½ cup (112 g) of the salt and sugar and stir until dissolved. Cool the brine to room temperature and then transfer to a 2-quart (1.9 L) container and refrigerate until cold, at least 2 hours. Add the fish to the brine and refrigerate for 1 to 2 hours.

While the fish is brining, preheat your smoker to 250°F (121°C). About 30 minutes before you are ready to cook, stoke the fire with hardwood; we prefer alder or oak for this. (See page 212 for additional information on preparing a smoker.)

Remove the fish from the brine and pat it dry with paper towels. Insert a probe thermometer into the fish, place in the smoker, and smoke to an internal temperature of 140°F (60°C), 10 to 25 minutes, depending on the thickness of the fillet. Transfer the fish to a plate and refrigerate until cold, about 30 minutes.

While the fish is chilling, combine the yogurt, sour cream, shallots, pepper, remaining 1 teaspoon of salt, and Old Bay in a bowl and whisk together. Flake the fish into the bowl and fold it into the yogurt mixture.

Serve with Asiago Black Pepper Crackers for dipping.

STORAGE

Refrigerate in a tightly sealed container for up 3 days.

ASIAGO BLACK PEPPER CRACKERS

ACTIVE TIME: 30 MINUTES
TOTAL TIME: 1 HOUR 30 MINUTES
YIELD: ABOUT 80 PIECES

INGREDIENTS

- 2 cups (160 g) shredded Asiago cheese
- 1 cup (125 g) all-purpose flour
- ½ cup (56 g) almond flour
- ½ cup (112 g) chilled unsalted butter, diced
- 1 tablespoon (4 g) minced fresh dill
- 1 teaspoon kosher salt
- 1 teaspoon coarsely ground black pepper
- ½ teaspoon dried thyme
- ½ teaspoon ground nutmeg
- 2 to 3 tablespoons (28 to 45 ml) whole milk

SPECIAL EQUIPMENT

- Parchment paper
- Food processor

METHOD

Preheat the oven to 350°F (180°C, or gas mark 4). Line a sheet pan with parchment paper.

Combine the Asiago cheese, flours, butter, and seasonings in a food processor bowl and sprinkle with 2 tablespoons (28 ml) of the milk. Pulse about 5 times and then process until the mixture starts to clump, 8 to 10 seconds. Pinch a bit of the dough; if it is dry and crumbly, add milk, 1 teaspoon (5 ml) at a time, to form a moist but not sticky dough.

Place the dough on a lightly floured work surface and pat into a ½-inch (1.3 cm)-thick disk. Use a rolling pin to roll it out gently until it is ⅛ inch (3 mm) thick. Cut the dough into 2-inch (5 cm)-wide strips and then cut each strip crosswise into ½-inch (1.3 cm)-wide bars. Transfer to the parchment-lined sheet pan, spacing the crackers about 1 inch (2.5 cm) apart. Reroll the scraps to create more crackers until all the dough is used.

Bake in the center of the oven until the crackers are just starting to color and are firm to the touch, 18 to 20 minutes. They should be golden brown on the bottom. Allow to cool on the sheet pan.

STORAGE

Store in a tightly sealed container at room temperature for up to 5 days.

MAC AND CHEESE BALLS

ACTIVE TIME: 1 HOUR 45 MINUTES
TOTAL TIME: 2 HOURS 45 MINUTES
SERVES: 10 TO 12 (30 PIECES)

INGREDIENTS

- 6 ounces (170 g) uncooked bacon, diced (about 1 cup [225 g])
- 10 ounces (280 g) elbow macaroni
- ⅔ cup (179 g) Velveeta Cheese Sauce
- 1 teaspoon kosher salt, plus more for sprinkling
- ¾ cup (20 g) roughly chopped baby spinach
- ½ cup (58 g) shredded cheddar cheese
- 3 large eggs, beaten until well blended, divided
- 2 cups (250 g) all-purpose flour, divided
- 2 cups (230 g) seasoned dry breadcrumbs
- 6 cups (1.4 L) vegetable oil, for frying
- BBQ Ranch (page 198), for serving

SPECIAL EQUIPMENT

- Parchment paper
- Deep-fry thermometer

IF YOU WANT THESE TO SOUND FANCIER, YOU COULD CALL THEM AMERICAN ARANCINI, AFTER THE STUFFED ITALIAN RICE BALLS. BUT WE'VE NEVER HAD ANY TROUBLE MARKETING THEM. THIS IS FRIED MAC AND CHEESE. WITH BACON. AND BBQ RANCH. (WILL'S MOTTO IS "RANCH GOES WITH EVERYTHING.") THESE CAN BE SHAPED A COUPLE OF DAYS IN ADVANCE—THE KITCHEN MIGHT GET A LITTLE MESSY—AND FRIED JUST BEFORE YOUR GUESTS ARRIVE.

METHOD

Line a sheet pan with parchment paper.

Cook the bacon in a skillet over medium heat, stirring occasionally, until crisp. Drain well and set aside.

Cook the macaroni just past al dente according to package directions. Drain well and transfer to a medium mixing bowl. Stir in the cheese sauce, bacon, and salt and cool for 5 minutes. Fold in the spinach and cheddar cheese. Add 2 tablespoons (28 ml) of the beaten eggs and ½ cup (63 g) of the flour; mix until thoroughly blended. Take 1 heaping tablespoon (15 ml) of the mixture and squeeze it firmly in your hand to form a tight ball; repeat to form about 30 balls and arrange them on the parchment-lined sheet pan. Cover loosely with plastic wrap and chill for at least 20 minutes or overnight.

To bread the mac and cheese balls, place 3 small mixing bowls on a work surface. Place the remaining 1½ cups (188 g) of flour in 1 bowl, the remaining eggs in the next bowl, and the breadcrumbs in the last bowl. One at a time, compact a ball in your hands again and coat it lightly in the flour and then in the egg, allowing the excess to drip off. Finally, roll the ball in the breadcrumbs, pressing gently so they adhere. Return the breaded ball to the sheet pan and repeat with the remaining balls. Cover the pan lightly with plastic wrap and refrigerate until you are ready to fry.

Attach a deep-fry thermometer to the side of a large heavy-bottomed pan and add oil to a depth of 1 inch (2.5 cm). Place the pan over medium-high heat. Place a paper towel–lined sheet pan beside the stove.

CONTINUED

When the oil reaches 360°F (182°C), carefully transfer the mac and cheese balls to the oil, working in batches to avoid crowding the pan. Fry until golden brown, about 2 minutes per side, and transfer to the paper towel–lined pan to drain. Sprinkle lightly with salt.

Let cool for a few minutes before serving with the BBQ Ranch.

STORAGE

Refrigerate the uncooked mac and cheese balls in a tightly sealed container for up to 5 days. Freeze uncooked mac and cheese balls for up to 1 month. Defrost before frying.

BBQ RANCH

ACTIVE TIME: 15 MINUTES
TOTAL TIME: 20 MINUTES
YIELD: 2 CUPS (420 G)

INGREDIENTS

- 1 medium carrot, peeled and cut into chunks
- 1 stalk celery, cut into 4 pieces
- ¾ cup (175 g) mayonnaise
- ¾ cup (175 ml) whole buttermilk
- 2 teaspoons kosher salt
- 2 teaspoons coarsely ground black pepper
- 2 teaspoons garlic powder
- 1 teaspoon onion powder
- 2 tablespoons (28 ml) Bare-Bones BBQ Sauce (page 35)

SPECIAL EQUIPMENT

- Food processor

METHOD

Finely mince the carrot in a food processor; you should have about ¼ cup (28 g). Transfer to a small bowl. Repeat with the celery, transfer to a few layers of paper towel, and squeeze dry; you should have ¼ cup (30 mg). Add to the carrots.

Combine the mayonnaise, buttermilk, salt, and spices in the processor and pulse to blend. Allow to sit for 5 minutes. Pulse in the BBQ sauce until incorporated and then the vegetables.

STORAGE

Refrigerate in a tightly sealed container for up to 3 days.

PORK BELLY BÁNH MÌ

ACTIVE TIME: 45 MINUTES
TOTAL TIME: 45 MINUTES
SERVES: 10 TO 12

WILL MADE THESE FOR A HOLIDAY PARTY A FEW YEARS AGO AND THEY WERE SUCH A HIT, THEY'VE BECOME A NEW TRADITION. BÁNH MÌ ISN'T A FAMILIAR SIGHT ON MOST AMERICAN HOLIDAY BUFFETS, BUT THE LIGHTLY PICKLED VEGETABLES AND FRESH HERBS MAKE THE VIETNAMESE SANDWICH STAND OUT AGAINST THE RICH DISHES OF THE SEASON.

INGREDIENTS

- 4 medium carrots, coarsely shredded (about 3 cups [330 g])
- ½ English cucumber, sliced (about 2 cups [238 g])
- 4 ounces (115 g) daikon, thinly shaved (about 1 cup [116 g])
- 8 radishes, thinly sliced (about ½ cup [58 g])
- ¼ cup (40 g) julienned red onion
- 1 small jalapeño pepper, seeded and thinly sliced into rings (about ⅓ cup [23 g])
- 3 cloves garlic, thinly sliced
- 3 tablespoons (36 g) sugar
- 1 tablespoon (14 g) kosher salt
- ¼ cup (60 ml) rice wine vinegar
- Juice of 1 lime
- 2 tablespoons (28 ml) fish sauce
- 1 cup (225 g) mayonnaise
- 2 tablespoons (28 ml) sriracha
- 10 to 12 mini (6 inches, or 15 cm each) baguettes or sub rolls
- 1¼ cups (260 g) liver mousse (optional; see Ingredient Guide, page 217)
- 1 batch Pork Belly Burnt Ends (page 165)
- 1 bunch fresh mint sprigs
- 1 bunch fresh cilantro sprigs

METHOD

Toss the carrots, cucumber, daikon, radishes, red onion, jalapeño, and garlic in a large mixing bowl until incorporated. Mix in the sugar and salt and let sit for 5 minutes. Add the vinegar, lime juice, and fish sauce and let the vegetables sit for at least 10 minutes more. Drain.

Mix together the mayonnaise and sriracha in a medium bowl.

To assemble the bánh mì, slice each roll horizontally halfway through and spread open like a book. Spread about 2 tablespoons (28 g) of liver mousse on the bottom half of the roll, if using, and spread about 1 tablespoon (15 g) of sriracha mayonnaise on the top half. Pile about ¾ cup (113 g) of the pork belly over the mousse and top with ⅓ to ½ cup (50 to 75 g) pickled vegetables. Garnish with the mint and cilantro.

STORAGE

Refrigerate the pickled vegetables in a tightly sealed container for up to 3 days. Refrigerate the sriracha mayo in a tightly sealed container for up to 5 days.

SAL'S BOUDIN BALLS

ACTIVE TIME: 2 HOURS
TOTAL TIME: 4 HOURS TO OVERNIGHT
SERVES: 10 TO 12 (24 PIECES)

INGREDIENTS

- 5 cups (1.2 L) water
- 10 ounces (280 g) pork butt, cut into 1-inch (2.5 cm) cubes
- 4 ounces (115 g) chicken livers
- ¼ cup (40 g) diced yellow onion
- ¼ cup (38 g) diced green bell pepper
- 1 stalk celery, diced
- 1½ teaspoons kosher salt, divided, plus more for sprinkling
- 1 teaspoon coarsely ground black pepper, divided
- ½ teaspoon cayenne pepper
- ¾ cup (135 g) uncooked jasmine rice
- 2 tablespoons (8 g) roughly chopped parsley
- 2 tablespoons (12 g) thinly sliced scallion greens
- 2 cups (100 g) panko breadcrumbs, divided
- 6 cups (1.4 L) vegetable oil, for frying
- Dijon mustard, for serving

SPECIAL EQUIPMENT

- Food processor
- Fine-mesh strainer
- Deep-fry thermometer

THIS RECIPE COMES FROM SAL FRISTINSKY, A NEW YORK CITY FIREMAN FROM HARLEM WHO OWNS SOME RATHER NOTORIOUS BARS IN BROOKLYN. IN A PREVIOUS LIFE, SAL WORKED WITH ANDY AND THEY COOKED THIS SWEET, SPICY, CRUNCHY DISH TOGETHER ONE TIME AT THE RENOWNED JAMES BEARD HOUSE. YOU HAVE TO PROMISE YOU WON'T LET THE CHICKEN LIVERS PUT YOU OFF THIS. THIS IS THE BITE THAT WILL CONVINCE YOU THAT YOU LOVE LIVER.

METHOD

Combine the water, pork, chicken livers, onion, green pepper, celery, 1 teaspoon (5 g) of the salt, ½ teaspoon of the black pepper, and the cayenne pepper in a medium saucepan. Bring to a boil and then adjust the heat to a simmer; cook until the pork is very tender, about 1 hour. Strain, reserving the liquid and solids separately. Cool the meat mixture to room temperature.

Heat 1½ cups (355 ml) of the strained cooking liquid in a clean saucepan over high heat. Bring to a boil and add the rice; stir well, adjust the heat to a simmer, and cook, partly covered, until the rice is tender, about 18 minutes. Set aside to cool.

Pulse the cooled meat in a food processor to form a fluffy mousse. Scrape into a medium bowl and add the cooked rice, parsley, scallions, remaining ½ teaspoon (3 g) of salt, and remaining ½ teaspoon of black pepper, or to taste. The mixture should be moist; if it seems dry, add a few tablespoons (28 to 45 ml) of the remaining cooking liquid. It should be creamy, but not wet. Refrigerate until cold and firm, 4 hours or overnight.

Pulse 1 cup (50 g) of the panko in a food processor until finely ground. Transfer to a medium bowl and add the remaining 1 cup (50 g) of panko. Toss until evenly mixed and set aside.

Divide the mixture into twenty-four 1-ounce (28 g) balls (about 1 heaping tablespoon each). Roll the balls in the panko and transfer to a sheet pan.

Attach a deep-fry thermometer to the side of a large heavy-bottomed pan and add oil to a depth of 1½ inches (3.8 cm). Place the pan over medium-high heat. Place a paper towel–lined sheet pan beside the stove.

When the oil reaches 350°F (180°C), carefully transfer the balls to the oil, working in batches to avoid crowding the pan. Fry, turning occasionally, until well browned and firm, 5 to 6 minutes. (Do not undercook or the balls will be too soft to hold their shape.) Transfer the finished balls to the paper towel–lined pan to drain; sprinkle lightly with salt. Cool for a few minutes before serving with Dijon mustard.

STORAGE

Refrigerate uncooked boudin balls in a tightly sealed container for up to 1 day.

HOPPIN' JOHN

⏰ **ACTIVE TIME:** 30 MINUTES
TOTAL TIME: 1 HOUR
SERVES: 10 TO 12

THIS NEW YEAR'S DAY DISH IS SUPPOSED TO BRING GOOD LUCK TO ALL WHO EAT IT—AND WHAT PARTY HOST DOESN'T WANT A LITTLE LUCK? THE BLACK EYES OF THE PEAS PROMISE COINS TO FILL YOUR POCKETS AND THE SPINACH REPRESENTS CASH. PLUS, IT'S JUST A TASTY COMBINATION. WILL GREW UP EATING THIS TRADITIONAL SOUTHERN DISH AND SKIPPIN' JENNY—THE NAME GIVEN TO THE LEFTOVERS, IF YOU HAVE ANY.

INGREDIENTS

- 2 cups (370 g) uncooked Carolina Gold Rice or long-grain rice
- 3 cups (700 ml) water
- 2 tablespoons (28 g) kosher salt, divided
- 2 cans (15 ounces, or 425 g each) of black-eyed peas, rinsed and drained
- 8 ounces (225 g) thick-sliced raw bacon, cut crosswise into ½-inch (1.3 cm) strips
- 1 medium yellow onion, diced (about 2 cups [320 g])
- 6 cloves garlic, minced
- 3 stalks celery, diced (about 1 cup [120 g])
- 1 small green bell pepper, diced (about 1 cup [150 g])
- 2 cups (60 g) baby spinach
- 2 teaspoons fresh thyme leaves

METHOD

Rinse the rice in cold water until the water runs clear. Place the 3 cups (700 ml) of water, rice, and 1 tablespoon (14 g) of the salt in a medium saucepan over medium heat. Cover the pan. Bring to a boil and then reduce the heat to a simmer and cook for 15 minutes. All the water will be absorbed. Fold in the beans and cover to keep warm.

In a large sauté pan, cook the bacon over medium heat until crispy, about 5 minutes. Pour off all but 1 tablespoon (15 ml) of bacon grease. Add the onion, garlic, and remaining 1 tablespoon (14 g) of salt. Cook, stirring, until the onions are translucent and just starting to color, about 5 minutes. Raise the heat to high and add the celery, green bell pepper, and baby spinach, stirring until the spinach wilts and most of the liquid has evaporated, about 3 minutes. Stir in the thyme and then fold in the rice and beans.

STORAGE

Refrigerate in a tightly sealed container for up to 4 days.

CAVIAR WITH BBQ POTATO CHIPS

ACTIVE TIME: 20 MINUTES
TOTAL TIME: 20 MINUTES
SERVES: 10 TO 12

INGREDIENTS

- 1 batch Basic Pork BBQ Rub (page 32)
- ¼ teaspoon hickory powder (see ingredient Guide, page 217)
- 1 batch Homemade Potato Chips (page 178)
- 1 cup crème fraîche (224 g) or (230 g) sour cream
- About 8 ounces (225 g) caviar

CAVIAR ALWAYS FEELS ELEGANT, BUT IT DOESN'T HAVE TO BE INTIMIDATING. INSTEAD OF THE EXPECTED BLINI (A DELICATE BUCKWHEAT PANCAKE), WE SERVE THESE SALTY LITTLE JEWELS WITH SOMETHING EVERYONE KNOWS AND LOVES: HOMEMADE BBQ CHIPS. CRÈME FRAÎCHE IS THE TRADITIONAL—AND DELICIOUS—GARNISH, BUT, WELL, WE'RE BARBECUE GUYS. WE HAVE TO RECOMMEND YOU TOP IT WITH SOME SOUR CREAM.

METHOD

Combine the rub and hickory powder in a small bowl. Use the mixture to dust the Homemade Potato Chips.

Serve with sour cream and caviar.

HOW TO SERVE CAVIAR

These tips come from Jeremy Sewall, chef and restaurateur.

KNOW YOUR OPTIONS.
True Russian caviar is sturgeon eggs cured in salt. But that's not the only option. Salmon, trout, paddlefish, hackleback, and whitefish eggs from many places in the world are all delicious alternatives.

START SIMPLE.
Caviar can get expensive. If you are just learning about it, start with more economical options like paddlefish or hackleback. And remember: Imported is not always better. "California produces a lot of caviar," Jeremy says, "and most of it is really good quality at a good value."

TURN TO THE EXPERTS.
Jeremy relies on Island Creek, Marky's, and D'Artagnan—sources that can answer your questions and sell a lot of caviar. "Caviar is cured and has a decent shelf life, but it is seafood," Jeremy says. "Eat it fresh."

DON'T USE A METAL SPOON.
Caviar can absorb metallic flavors, so it is traditionally served with a mother-of-pearl spoon. But a plastic utensil will work just as well.

DO BREAK ALL THE OTHER RULES.
"When I think of caviar, my mind always goes to the classic presentation with crème fraîche, sieved eggs, onion, and blini," Jeremy says. "But it can be enjoyed in your backyard on a chip or in a sauce just as much as when sipping champagne."

CHOCOLATE BOURBON TRUFFLES

ACTIVE TIME: 25 MINUTES

TOTAL TIME: 2 HOURS OR 1 TO 2 DAYS

SERVES: 10 TO 12 (24 PIECES)

INGREDIENTS

- 5 ounces (140 g) brownies
- 24 chocolate wafer cookies or 9 chocolate graham crackers
- 1 cup (110 g) toasted, chopped pecans
- ¼ cup plus 3 tablespoons (53 g) confectioners' sugar, divided
- ¼ cup (60 ml) bourbon
- ¼ cup (78 g) sweetened condensed milk

SPECIAL EQUIPMENT

- Food processor

WARNING: THESE ARE A 21-AND-OVER DESSERT. THEY PACK A WALLOP OF BOURBON, THE PERFECT COMPLEMENT FOR CHOCOLATE AND PECANS. YOU CAN USE HOME-MADE BROWNIES HERE OR MAKE IT A NO-BAKE DISH WITH STORE-BOUGHT TREATS. PLAN AT LEAST A COUPLE OF HOURS—OR EVEN A COUPLE OF DAYS—TO LET THE FLAVORS MELD.

METHOD

Crumble the brownies and allow to dry overnight. Pulse in a food processor to form fine crumbs. You should have about 1 cup (140 g). Transfer to a bowl.

Pulse the cookies or graham crackers in a food processor to form fine crumbs. You should have about 1¼ cups (105 g). Add to the bowl of brownie crumbs, along with the pecans.

Sift 3 tablespoons (23 g) of the confectioners' sugar over the crumbs and stir until evenly mixed. Add the bourbon and stir to moisten the dry ingredients. Drizzle about half of the sweetened condensed milk over the mixture, stirring until mostly combined, and then add the remaining milk and stir until the texture is uniform. Let the mixture sit for 20 to 30 minutes for easier shaping.

Put the remaining ¼ cup (30 g) of confectioners' sugar on a plate or small bowl. Divide the dough into 24 balls, about 1 heaping tablespoon (20 g) each. Roll the balls between your palms until they are smooth and shiny, then roll in the confectioners' sugar one at a time, and transfer to a plate.

Let the balls sit at room temperature for at least 2 hours (or overnight in the refrigerator) to allow the flavors to meld. Serve at room temperature.

STORAGE

Refrigerate in a tightly sealed container for up to 6 days.

MAKE YOUR OWN 'NOG

ACTIVE TIME: 45 MINUTES

TOTAL TIME: 4 HOURS

SERVES: 10 TO 12

INGREDIENTS

- 6 cups (1.4 L) whole milk
- 2 cups (475 ml) heavy cream
- ¼ cup (60 ml) maple syrup
- 1 teaspoon ground nutmeg
- 1 teaspoon ground cardamom
- ½ teaspoon ground cinnamon
- 1 teaspoon kosher salt
- 8 large eggs yolks
- 1 cup (200 g) sugar
- Your favorite bourbon (optional)

THE EGGNOG YOU BUY AT THE GROCERY STORE? THAT'S NOT THIS. HOMEMADE EGG-NOG IS A WHOLE DIFFERENT EXPERIENCE, ONE THAT IS WELL WORTH THE STIRRING TIME. THE EGGNOG IS A STUNNER ALL ON ITS OWN, BUT ANDY SERVES HIS ALONGSIDE A SELECTION OF WHISKEY. HIS FAVORITES INCLUDE ANGEL'S ENVY, SAGAMORE RYE, AND WHISTLEPIG, AND HE SUGGESTS LOTS OF BROWN LIQUOR WITH JUST A SPLASH OF 'NOG.

METHOD

Combine the milk, heavy cream, maple syrup, spices, and salt in medium sauce-pan. Bring to a simmer over medium heat and cook for 5 minutes, stirring continually; do not let the milk boil. Remove from the heat and let stand for 5 minutes.

Set up an ice bath: Fill a deep bowl halfway with ice water and set a large, shallow bowl on top.

Whisk the egg yolks and sugar in a medium bowl until uniformly blended. Gradually drizzle in 2 cups (475 ml) of the hot liquid, whisking until the sugar is dissolved. Return the egg mixture to the saucepan, whisking to blend.

Return the saucepan to medium heat and stir continually until it thickens enough to coat the back of a spoon; do not let it boil. Pour into the prepared ice bath and stir continually until cool. (This will stop the eggs from cooking and thickening the eggnog too much.) Cover and refrigerate until cold, about 3 hours.

Let your guests add bourbon to their tastes.

STORAGE

Cover and refrigerate for up to 4 days.

THE SMOKE SHOP BASICS

MOST OF WHAT WE DO IS BARBECUE—THAT IS, SMOKING FOOD OVER INDIRECT HEAT USING CHARCOAL AND HARDWOOD.

YOU DON'T NEED FANCY EQUIPMENT TO MAKE GREAT BARBECUE. WE'VE OWNED AND OPERATED MANY DIFFERENT TYPES OF SMOKERS OVER THE YEARS, FROM HOMEMADE BARREL COOKERS TO $15,000 TRAILER RIGS, AND THERE HAVE BEEN PLENTY OF TIMES WHEN OUR FOOD IS JUST AS AMAZING COMING OFF OUR INEXPENSIVE EQUIPMENT AS IT IS FROM OUR CUSTOM PIECE. THE PIT MASTER IS ALWAYS MORE IMPORTANT THAN THE PIT.

IF YOU ARE JUST GETTING STARTED, HERE ARE A FEW OPTIONS.

VERTICAL SMOKERS

In vertical smokers, the charcoal fire sits directly beneath the grates holding the food being cooked. Generally, a water pan or metal plate acts as a heat buffer between the fire and the meat and allows for indirect cooking. Airflow is restricted by adjustable vents, to allow the charcoal and wood to burn steady and slow.

The gold standard of inexpensive, highly functional vertical cookers is the Weber Smokey Mountain (WSM). Numerous other smoker manufacturers that follow this basic design include the popular (but more expensive) Big Green Egg, Backwoods Smokers, and Spicewine Ironworks.

PREPARING A VERTICAL SMOKER:

1 Clean it. Remove any ash or old charcoal from inside the smoker.

2 If your smoker does not have a built-in thermometer, place a probe or oven thermometer on the grill grate. (A good trick is to insert the probe into half a potato.)

3 Fill the charcoal area almost to capacity with unlit lump charcoal.

4 Outside the smoker, fill a charcoal chimney with hardwood lump charcoal, crumple two pieces of newspaper and stuff them below the coals, and light the newspaper. Wait about 10 minutes for the charcoal to become fully ignited. Flames should just be starting to peek through the top of the pile.

5 Carefully, wearing heatproof gloves, pour the lit charcoal evenly over the bed of unlit charcoal inside the smoker.

6 Fill the water pan with cold water. Or, if the recipe calls for smoking in the 300°F to 400°F (150°C to 200°C) range, leave the water pan empty. Make sure the pan is very clean and line it with foil to make cleanup easy.

7 Depending on the type of vertical smoker you are using, either close the doors or cover with the smoker lid. Open the top and bottom vents completely.

8 When the temperature inside the smoker reaches 250°F (121°C), remove the lid and clean the grill grates with a brush. Now is the time to stoke the fire with "smoke wood"—two or three fist-size chunks of dry hardwood as recommended by the recipe.

9 Close the smoker and let it return to the target temperature your recipe calls for.

10 Add the food to be cooked and allow the smoker to return to the target temperature.

11 Close the bottom vents by three-quarters.

12 Adjust the bottom vents to maintain the temperature. Close them slightly to lower the temperature; open them slightly to raise the temperature.

13 If the temperature runs too hot, close the top vent by half. This will bring the temperature down.

14 Add water to the water pan every 3 to 4 hours, if using.

15 A full load of charcoal should be enough fuel for most cooking sessions. But keep an eye on how much charcoal is being used and add more as needed to maintain your target temperature.

OFFSET SMOKERS

Offset smokers feature a long horizontal cooking chamber sitting next to a firebox. These range from a small $500 model available at hardware stores (which we do not recommend) to enormous, heavy steel models costing upward of $15,000. Typically, these latter constructions are custom-made in the southern United States, like the Jambo Pit.

Where vertical smokers use predominantly hardwood lump charcoal, offset smokers take a base of charcoal, but are primarily fueled by wood logs. And while the airflow is constrained in the vertical smokers, the offset smoker depends on powerful airflow to keep a log fire burning and to heat up all that steel.

The offset smoker provides a simpler, more primal, hands-on approach to smoking food. While vertical smokers can be left unattended for several hours, their offset counterparts require babysitting and playing with fire—which we think is a good thing. It gives us a good excuse to sit in our lawn chairs with a cooler of beer.

PREPARING AN OFFSET SMOKER:

1 Clean out all the ash from the firebox.

2 If your smoker does not have a built-in thermometer, place a probe or oven thermometer on the grill grate. (A good trick is to insert the probe into half a potato.)

3 Create a base of lump charcoal and pour a chimney of lit charcoal (see directions for vertical smoker) into the firebox.

4 Place three splits of dry firewood over the charcoal fire, stacked like a tepee. Close the firebox door only when the wood is actively burning.

5 Once the temperature inside the smoker reaches 250°F (121°C), open the doors and clean the grill grates with a brush.

6 Add the food to be cooked and let the smoker return to the temperature stipulated in the recipe.

7 Ideally, you should keep all vents completely open and control the temperature of your pit with the size of the fire. If the smoker is running too hot, you can close the vents temporarily, but try to keep the vents completely open as much of the time as possible.

8 Add a new log roughly every hour to maintain a steady temperature and a good base of coals. If the fire burns down too much, add more lump charcoal to rebuild your base and then add another log.

KETTLE GRILLS

Kettle grills are probably the most common piece of charcoal-fired outdoor cooking equipment. You can cook almost all the recipes in this book with a 22-inch (55 cm) kettle grill. There are many ways to use them. For smoking, we prefer the two-zone fire approach, in which a fire is built on one side of the kettle. This allows for grilling close to the fire and gives the pit master the flexibility to move the food to the cooler side of the grill to finish cooking, if needed.

PREPARING A KETTLE GRILL:

1 Pour some hardwood lump charcoal so it piles up against one side of the kettle.

2 Fill a chimney half full. Use crumpled newspaper to get the fire started (see directions for vertical smoker).

3 Pour the lit charcoal over the pile of unlit charcoal. One side of the grill should now have an active charcoal fire going and the other side should have no charcoal at all.

4 Open the lid and remove the grill grate. Stoke the fire with a couple of chunks of hardwood, as directed by the recipe, and place a disposable baking pan next to the fire. Replace the grill grate and place the meat directly over the baking pan. Close the lid and position the exhaust vent away from the fire so the smoke is drawn across and over the meat. Adjust the bottom vents so they are three-quarters closed. Add more charcoal every 1 to 2 hours, rotating the meat to ensure even cooking.

GENERAL TIPS FOR SUCCESS

→ Calibrate your thermometer. Fill a glass with ice water. Submerge the tip of the thermometer in the water. It should read 32°F (0°C). If it doesn't, adjust it according to the manufacturer's instructions. Or, treat yourself to a new thermometer.

→ Monitor the grate temperature of the cooker with a calibrated probe thermometer. Temperatures can vary quite a bit from the grate to the exhaust; always monitor the temperatures close to the foods you are smoking.

→ Never use lighter fluid—unless you want your food to taste like gasoline. A charcoal chimney is all you need.

→ Make sure your wood supply is dry and has been aged for at least six months. It should burn easily and not smolder. And never soak wood in water. Wet wood will smolder and the fire will not burn clean. Good airflow that allows the chunks of wood to actively combust instead of smolder is key. Without active combustion, creosote will be created. This thick, oily substance produces a bitter flavor and dark, burnt-looking meats.

→ When getting started, err on the side of using not enough hardwood, rather than too much. Later, when you have more experience, you can add more to suit your taste. We find guests enjoy a mild hint of smoke that does not dominate the flavor profile of the food.

→ Burn a clean fire. A clean fire will produce a sweet smoke flavor and more of a ruby red color on meats. You know you have a clean fire when all you can see coming out of the exhaust is a thin blue line of smoke. White, billowing puffs of smoke mean you are not ready to cook yet. Black smoke means your smoker is not clean—or your food is on fire. A completely open top exhaust vent encourages a clean fire. Only close it to lower the temperature if you overshoot the target significantly for what you are cooking.

→ Be patient when adjusting the vents to change the cooker temperature. Make small tweaks and wait 20 to 30 minutes to check the results. If the temperature is still not quite where you need it to be, make another adjustment. Temperature changes should be slow and steady, without spikes.

→ Settle in. Some recipes have long cooking times. That's part of the fun.

INGREDIENT GUIDE

ACTIVATED CHARCOAL POWDER

This is a fine, odorless, black powder; small amounts can be used as a food coloring.
Available at: Natural food stores or pharmacies

ALEPPO PEPPER

Common in Middle Eastern cuisine, the dried, ground Halaby pepper is slightly hot with earthy and fruity flavors.
Available at: The Spice House (www.thespicehouse.com) or your favorite spice retailer

COTIJA CHEESE

This is a hard crumbly Mexican cheese typically made with cow's milk.
Available at: Hispanic grocery stores

DRIED CHILE DE ÀRBOL

This is a hot pepper with a nutty flavor often used in Mexican cuisine.
Available at: The Spice House (www.thespicehouse.com) or your favorite spice retailer

EPAZOTE

This is an aromatic herb often used in Mexican cuisine.
Available at: The Spice House (www.thespicehouse.com) or your favorite spice retailer

ESPELETTE PEPPER

This is a mild pepper that is often used in Basque cuisine.
Available at: The Spice House (www.thespicehouse.com) or your favorite spice retailer

GUAJILLO PEPPERS

Common in Mexican cuisine, the dried mirasol pepper has a medium heat and a slight sweetness.
Available at: The Spice House (www.thespicehouse.com) or your favorite spice retailer

HICKORY POWDER

This is an alternative to liquid smoke.
Available at: The Spice House (www.thespicehouse.com) or your favorite spice retailer

JUNIPER BERRIES

The cone of a juniper tree, it has a resinous flavor and is often an ingredient in gin.
Available at: The Spice House (www.thespicehouse.com) or your favorite spice retailer

KEWPIE MAYONNAISE

This is a Japanese mayo that is smoother and creamier than the American version.
Available at: Asian grocery stores

KOMBU DASHI POWDER

This is a Japanese soup base made from dried kelp.
Available at: Asian grocery stores

LARD (*MANTECA*)

A soft white fat from pigs, it is known as *Manteca* in Mexico.
Available at: Hispanic grocery stores

LIVER MOUSSE

This is a thick, smooth pâté typically made of chicken or pork liver or a combination of the two.
Available at: Gourmet markets and Asian grocery stores

MAGGI SEASONING SAUCE

This is a savory condiment similar to soy sauce popular in many Asian cuisines.
Available at: Asian grocery stores

MUSHROOM POPCORN KERNELS

This popcorn is almost round when popped.
Available at: Just Poppin (shop.justpoppin.com)

NUTRITIONAL YEAST

A deactivated yeast described as nutty, cheesy, or creamy, it is popular as a vegan condiment.
Available at: Natural food stores

OAXACA CHEESE

This is a semi-hard Mexican cheese with the texture of string cheese.
Available at: Hispanic grocery stores

PORCINI POWDER

Dried and ground porcini mushrooms, used to add umami flavors to a dish.
Available at: The Spice House (www.thespicehouse.com) or your favorite spice retailer

PRAGUE POWDER #1 (AKA PINK CURING SALT)

This is a common curing salt, made of sodium nitrate and table salt.
Available at: The Spice House (www.thespicehouse.com) or your favorite spice retailer

SILVER AND GOLD EDIBLE FOIL

This is a glittering but flavorless garnish made from actual silver and gold.
Available at: Barnabas Blattgold (www.barnabasgold.com) and most pastry supply shops

SZECHUAN PEPPERCORNS

Popular in Szechuan cuisine, this seed causes a tingly sensation in the mouth.
Available at: The Spice House (www.thespicehouse.com) or your favorite spice retailer

THANK QS

ANDY AND WILL WOULD LIKE TO THANK

The entire Smoke Shop team for their hard work and endless dedication to excellence in BBQ and hospitality.

April White for her incredible writing and vision for this book.

Nancy Kohl for recipe development and testing. Your ability to take our ideas and make them work on a practical level is pure magic. This book would not be what it is without you.

Chris Hart and Andrea Pyenson for recipe development.

Minister of Beverage Michael Boughton for his crazy good cocktails and bourbon knowledge.

Brian Lesser for his partnership and leadership.

The team at Quarto: Thom O'Hearn, Regina Grenier, and Winnie Prentiss. We loved working with you and we appreciate all that you did for us and your help with the vision for this book.

Catrine Kelty for her astounding visual talents.

And a huge thank Q to all the other experts that lent their talents to this book and our parties. We couldn't have done it without you: Ronnie Savenor, Sarah McKnight, Taniya Nayak, Amy Mills, Garret Harker, Ken Goodman Photography, Jeremy Sewell, Franky Readon aka Franky Fumbles, and Sal Fristinsky.

ANDY WOULD ALSO LIKE TO THANK

My wife, Rice. Thank you for your love and support, you make life perfect.

The IQUE BBQ TEAM: The best pit master I know and team leader Chris Hart, Jamie Hart, Ed Doyle, John Delpha, Sal Fristinsky, Ernie Kim, Ken Goodman, and Mike Snow.

My mother, Harriet, and the Wales, the Denholtzes, and the Enriquezes.

Ken, you get another shout-out! We've been at this game since college and it's been a pleasure being your friend and working with you on five books. Your photography rocks.

A big thank Q to Chef Will. It's been a pleasure writing this book with you. And big love to the Team at Firemasters. Thank you Mike, Jen, Dylan, and the entire crew.

WILL WOULD ALSO LIKE TO THANK

My wife, Sarah. Thank you for showing me a world of endless happiness.

My mom and dad for letting me figure it out for myself.

Ian Grossman for giving me a legitimate reason for moving back to Boston.

Aliza Stern Grossman for taking a baking class.

Carrie and Michael Bergin, Louie Dibiccari, and the L'espalier/Sel de la Terre family.

Stephanie Izard and my extended Goat Family.

And a big thank Q to Chef Andy for giving me the opportunity to be a part of something great. It has been a wonderful experience writing this book with you. Thank you for your generosity and for teaching me how to write a cookbook.

ABOUT THE AUTHOR

ANDY HUSBANDS

ANDY HUSBANDS is the award-winning chef, author, and pitmaster behind The Smoke Shop, Boston's acclaimed barbecue restaurant, winner of "Best Barbecue" from *Boston Magazine* and *The Improper Bostonian*. With a career spanning nearly 30 years in the restaurant industry, Husbands serves as one of the city's most celebrated culinary leaders and foremost authority on regional barbecue and live-fire cooking in New England.

Born and raised in Seattle, Husbands relocated to New England with his family at age 14 and quickly found his calling in the kitchen, working at a neighborhood bakery in Needham, Massachusetts. After earning his degrees in culinary arts and hospitality management from Johnson & Wales University, Husbands went on to accept the sous chef position at the famed East Coast Grill in Cambridge, Massachusetts, under the helm of James Beard Award-winning chef Chris Schlesinger. It was here where

Husbands first developed a passion for live-fire cooking, and less than a year later, he was appointed executive chef.

Husbands has long been part of the Boston restaurant scene, with a 20-year career that includes opening mainstays of the city's South End, Tremont 647 and Sister Sorel. After two decades on the competitive barbecue circuit, Husbands debuted his newest concept, The Smoke Shop, opening its first location in Cambridge's Kendall Square in 2016. A long-time passion project for Husbands, The Smoke Shop culminates his years of practice, research, and continued success as a World Barbeque Champion, serving a menu that showcases his modern approach to slow-cooked, old school-style barbecue.

Hailed "Boston's Meat Maven" by the *Boston Globe*, Husbands first came into the national spotlight competing on Season 6 of FOX Television Network's fiery *Hell's Kitchen*, and has since appeared on *CBS This Morning*, *Food Network*, *Fox & Friends*, and most recently, *Cooking Channel's Burgers, Brew & 'Que*. He is the cofounder of the internationally-recognized barbecue team IQUE BBQ, which became the first New England team to win the World Champions of BBQ title in 2009 at the Jack Daniels World Championship in Tennessee. He has coauthored five cookbooks, including *Wicked Good Burgers*, *Wicked Good BBQ*, *Grill to Perfection*, *The Fearless Chef*, and *Pitmaster*, which was awarded "Book of the Year" by *National Barbeque News*.

Deeply rooted in the community, Husbands passionately drives awareness for Share Our Strength, the nation's leading childhood hunger relief organization, serving as honorary chair of its annual Taste of the Nation fundraiser. He is also an active board member of the Massachusetts Restaurant Association, for which he was honored as MRA's Chef of the Year in 2014, as well as a Rodman Celebration Restaurant Chair. In his spare time, Husbands enjoys volunteering at local organizations including Pine Street Inn and Rosie's Place, and, most importantly, spending time with his wife, Rice, and their twin girls, at their home in Stoneham, Massachusetts.

ABOUT THE AUTHOR

WILL SALAZAR

ABOUT THE PHOTOGRAPHER

KEN GOODMAN

Pitmaster **WILL SALAZAR** is chef de cuisine and director of day-to-day culinary operations at The Smoke Shop BBQ restaurants. Salazar studied culinary arts management at Johnson & Wales University and with a desire to broaden his education and skill set, went on to stage all over Europe, most notably at Guy Savoy and Taillievent. He first moved to Boston in 2001 to work under the tutelage of Geoff Gardner and Frank McClelland at L'Espalier and Sel de la Terre, where he rose to the position of chef de cuisine in 2007. After leaving Boston in 2010, Salazar spent the next two years in New York City before touring The US Virgin Islands, Argentina, and Chicago, where he served as a sous chef under Stephanie Izard at both Girl and the Goat and Little Goat.

After a four-year stint under Izard, Pitmaster Salazar was lured to The Smoke Shop, where his role is to further define Andy Husbands' vision of "City Q" and to help others master the craft of barbecue, which has become one of his favorite parts of the job. Salazar lives in East Cambridge, Massachusetts with his wife, Sarah, daughter, Amelia, and dog, Buster.

Photographer **Ken Goodman** is a freelance photographer based in NYC specializing in cookbooks, food, concerts and events. Prior to photography, he spent 20 great years in the restaurant industry as a classically trained chef with a culinary degree from Johnson & Wales University. He still satisfies his cooking vice as a member of the nationally ranked BBQ Team IQUE, past winners of the Jack Daniel's World Championship of Barbecue!

INDEX